SCRIPTURAL INSIGHTS AND COMMENTARY

The BOOK of MORMON

OTHER COVENANT BOOKS AND AUDIOBOOKS
BY TAYLOR HALVERSON, PhD

*Millions Shall Know Brother Joseph Again*

*Knowing Why: 137 Evidences That the Book of Mormon Is True*

*Scriptural Insights and Commentary: The New Testament*

SCRIPTURAL INSIGHTS AND COMMENTARY

# *The* BOOK *of* MORMON

TAYLOR HALVERSON, PhD

Covenant Communications, Inc.

Cover Images:

*The Risen Lord* © Arnold Friberg 2019. Used by permission from Creative Fine Art. For print information go to www.creativefineart.com. Uncropped image shown above.

*The First Vision* © J. Leo Fairbanks (1878–1946) | United States. Preliminary study, oil on board, year unknown, gift of Jonathan L. Fairbanks.

*Plate VIII: General View of Las Monjas, at Uxmal,* by Frederick Catherwood, *Views of Ancient Monuments in Central America, Chiapas and Yucatan,* 1844, London: Archivio White Star.

*Main Temple at Tulum,* by Frederick Catherwood, *Views of Ancient Monuments in Central America, Chiapas and Yucatan,* 1844, London: Archivio White Star.

Cover design copyright © 2019 by Covenant Communications, Inc.
Cover Design by Hannah Bischoff

Published by Covenant Communications, Inc.
American Fork, Utah

Printed in the United States of America
First Printing: October 2019

26 25 24 23 22 21 20 19    10 9 8 7 6 5 4 3 2 1

ISBN:978-1-52441-134-3

This book is dedicated to my maternal grandparents,
David John Ballstaedt and Helen Taylor Ballstaedt,
who instilled in me a love and veneration for Mormon as a
record keeper and as an observer and explainer of society.

# ACKNOWLEDGMENTS

Many people make a book possible. First, thanks goes to my wife, Lisa Rampton Halverson, who encouragingly supported me in this venture. For more than sixteen years, she has reviewed, edited, and provided insights on my writing.

I also feel deep appreciation to Dan Peterson, my former Arabic professor at Brigham Young University, who made it possible for me to publish many of these chapters on *Interpreter*. He also opened the door for me to write for the *Deseret News*.

I am grateful to the individuals at *Interpreter* who offered their time and assistance with many of my articles there: Debbie Peterson, Jeff Bradshaw, Allen Wyatt, Brant Gardner, and Ben McGuire. At the *Deseret News*, I thank Aaron Shill and Christine Rappleye for shepherding my writing there. At *LDS Living*, Jannalee Rosner Sandau and Danielle Beckstrom Wagner were sounding boards for great ideas, were thoughtful in their feedback, and were encouraging of the writing I put in front of them.

Many thanks go again to Scot and Maurine Proctor, who encouraged me and opened the first door for me to use my training in biblical studies to reach a larger audience through writing and publishing. I express appreciation for my coauthors and collaborators.

Finally, I share my heartfelt gratitude to my hundreds of thousands of readers on *Deseret News*, *LDS Living*, *Meridian*, my blog, and elsewhere who have shown interest in what I write and whose feedback has improved my thinking and writing. I write to you.

# SERIES INTRODUCTION

THIS IS THE SECOND BOOK in a four-volume set focused on scriptural insights and contexts.

Why another set of books about scripture? My hope is that those reading the chapters of this book will gain new enthusiasm and perspective for actually reading the scriptures, and not just for reading this book. I would be pleased if people just read the scriptures. But I know something of the excitement that fresh voices bring to entice us to delve back into the scriptures with renewed vigor and purpose. I know that from first-hand experience. And I wrote the articles in this book because of those first-hand personal experiences with other scripture lovers.

Some years ago, when I was fresh off my mission and working a summer job, I took to reading scholarship about the scriptures during my lunch breaks. The readings taught me, built me, expanded my understanding of scriptures in ways I was surprised to experience, having come off two years of intensive engagement with scripture. My study stirred deep motivations within me to learn, as the scholars had learned, about ancient history, peoples, cultures, and places. I wanted to read ancient literature, especially that which would expand my understanding about ancient Israel or the Bible. I felt a swelling desire to master the biblical languages of Hebrew and Greek. The book that set me on this journey was *Isaiah and the Prophets: Inspired Voices from the Old Testament* (1984), edited by Monte Nyman and Charles Tate, specifically the article in that book by Kent Jackson, "The Marriage of Hosea and Jehovah's Covenant with Israel." I found the book on my mom's bookshelf after I returned from my mission. She had received it as a gift from the CES coordinator in our area of Minnesota to say thank you for her many years of dedicated service teaching early-morning seminary. Little did I realize at that time, when I felt so deeply driven to learn, how those motivations would be eventually, paradoxically and simultaneously, diametrically deeply fulfilled and frustrated.

I decided to pursue the field of academic biblical scholarship as an undergraduate and graduate student. As I delved deeper into the Bible and the context of scripture, my appreciation for scripture grew in ways I had not anticipated. The beauty and ongoing sustaining power of scripture stunned me. These sacred texts had survived the test of time. These texts have been subjected to nearly every test and challenge humans could devise, and yet millions of us continue to find the texts endlessly useful and applicable in our lives. I came to love the scriptures more fully because I understood them more fully. As I knew better, my love and appreciation grew for these texts as it also grew for those who composed and transmitted these documents.

During all this time, my desire to share insights and perspectives with others expanded. I felt a burning desire to help the scriptures be more accessible, applicable, delightful, and engaging. I attempted to fulfill that desire by writing for others what I had found, sharing the excitement of discovering and explaining the meaning and significance.

Strangely, however, the very field that equipped me with tools, knowledge, perspective, and insight about the scriptures to bless the lives of others required that I use only my growing content expertise to gain more expertise and then share that with other content experts, not with regular people. With that context, I realized that no amount of content expertise with the scriptures and scripture scholarship would ever be a benefit to anyone else if I couldn't also share with those around me.

So I began writing.

Over several years I wrote a number of articles on select passages of the standard words of scriptures: The Old and New Testaments, Book of Mormon, Doctrine and Covenants, and The Pearl of Great Price. Some of these articles have been published in scattered locations. Now I bring together many of my scripture writings, published and unpublished, into a four-volume set.

My writings are not meant to be exhaustive. I share these articles as samples, hopefully delicious morsels of what a deeper study of select scripture passages can bring to one's soul. My hope is that as readers see how I read (in other words, interpret) scripture, they will gain new insights about their own scripture study.

My writing is informed by scholarship, but I am not writing to please a scholarly audience. I hope that scholars find something useful here. But my main intent is that all people will be delighted to dig deeper into the scriptures because of something I have written.

My hope is that this material will be informative, delightful, and engaging to readers. My hope is that readers will return to the scriptures with fresh energy to seek anew. I hope that as readers return to the scriptures, they will find renewal, refreshment, and answers to questions personal and mundane. And most importantly, I hope that my readers will feel the delight one can experience by studying scholarship and scriptures hand-in-hand.

Enjoy the read.

# BOOK INTRODUCTION

THIS BOOK BRINGS TOGETHER A variety of my writings about the Book of Mormon. Some chapters provide cultural background to the literary styles and doctrinal themes applied by Book of Mormon authors. Some chapters focus on a specific theme or doctrine; some of these chapters are shorter while others are longer, more in-depth treatments of a single topic. The book is arranged to move sequentially through the Book of Mormon, with more general articles clustering near the beginning and end of the book. For example, there is a chapter on the significance of the phrase "And it came to pass." Since this phrase is found throughout the Book of Mormon, it made the most sense to include that chapter near the beginning of the book.

As I have stated elsewhere, my hope is that through this book you will find renewed meaning and purpose in your scripture study; a broader perspective of the cultural, historical, thematic, and linguistic background for scripture; and an increasing love for these sacred texts. I also hope you will see that the Book of Mormon is an ancient, authentic scriptural text that was influenced by the culture and languages of the ancient Near East where its peoples originated. But most importantly, I hope my writings contribute to the truth that the Book of Mormon is a convincing witness that Jesus is the Christ.

My testimony of the Book of Mormon is simple. I hope that my words in this book will convince you to discover and experience anew that *the Book of Mormon is the most literarily beautiful, doctrinally truthful, and everlastingly applicable book the world has ever seen.*

**The Best Way to Get More Revelation in Your Life**[1]

Ask any typical Latter-day Saint, "Would you like more revelation in your life?" and the immediate answer will probably be "Yes!"

There are many ways to prepare for and to increase the likelihood of receiving revelation: repenting, singing hymns, offering more fervent prayer, attending the temple, forgiving others, finding solace in places of quiet (often in nature), being more mindful, learning, meditating, listening, and reading the scriptures.

Let's consider further this last suggestion of reading the scriptures. We remember that the Restoration began to roll forth because Joseph Smith did several things: he read from scriptures (James 1), he pondered what he read, he encountered a question that needed an answer, and he put that question to God in prayer.

Joseph Smith and Sidney Rigdon received the grand vision of the glories of heaven, now found in Doctrine and Covenants 76, because they had been reading John 5 in the New Testament.[2] They pondered what they read, which led to questions that needed to be answered. God delivered to them the panoramic view of the kingdoms of heaven in response to their questioning need.

What I find most striking about the principle of increasing our chances of revelation through scripture study is that the best example of this principle in action is Joseph Smith and the Book of Mormon.

Joseph Smith's reading of the Book of Mormon had more impact on his reception of revelation over a single three-month period than at any other time in his life. If you look at the list of dates when Joseph Smith's Doctrine and Covenants revelations occurred (look under "Chronological Order of Contents" near the beginning of the Doctrine and Covenants), you will see a significant clustering.

Between April and June 1829, Joseph received twelve revelations that are now canonized as part of the Doctrine and Covenants. Further review of the chronological list shows that there is no other three-month period in Joseph's entire prophetic career where he received more canonical revelations than during the April to June 1829 time period.

Why is that significant?

That three-month period from April to June 1829 is when Joseph Smith completed the bulk of the Book of Mormon translation/dictation process. In other words, Joseph Smith's reading of the Book of Mormon led to the greatest concentration of canonical revelations the Church has ever seen.

What would happen in our own lives if we spent more time reading the Book of Mormon, pondering what we read, finding questions about what we read, and asking those questions in search of answers? I believe that by reading the Book of Mormon more often we will find an abundance of light from above spreading into our hearts and lives that will quicken our understanding, increase our knowledge, help us draw closer to God, and fill our lives with unspeakable joy as we experience revealed truths in our personal lives.

## Unexpected Insights on the Meaning of Names and Titles for God in Scripture[3]

When we read the scriptures, many different words or titles are used for God. Some are used more than any others, and these names have special and significant meaning. Let's look at just a few of the names and titles for God used in scripture and the background behind them.

### God and Gods

If we could peel back the layers of the English text of the Bible and read in Hebrew, we'd be fascinated to learn that the familiar phrase, "In the beginning God [singular in English] created the heaven and the earth" actually reads in Hebrew, "In the beginning the Gods [plural in Hebrew] created the heaven and the earth" (Genesis 1:1).

Our modern-day scripture teaches this more correct reading: "the Gods, organized and formed the heavens and the earth" (Abraham 4:1).

Incidentally, the Hebrew word for *God* and the Arabic word for *God* both come from the same Semitic root word *Eloh*. We hear it as *Elohim* in Hebrew and *Allah* in Arabic.

What do we learn from this fact that the Hebrew text reads that Gods created the heavens and the earth?

First, we learn that God the Father is not alone. There are other Gods that assist Him in His creative work, including Heavenly Mother, God the Son, and God the Spirit. The Gospel of John teaches this principle: "In the beginning was the Word, and the Word was with God, and the Word was God. The same was in the beginning with God. All things were made by him; and without him was not any thing made that was made" (John 1:1–3).

Second, we learn that God's majesty is so magnificent and so beyond description that speaking of Him in the plural is natural. Though this example is inadequate to describe God's indomitable plurality, it gives us a taste of why it is natural for humans to speak in the plural about things that are so vast, expansive, and beyond our full experience. We all know what a desert is. But what do you call the world's largest desert? How about "deserts" (plural) to describe the unfathomable expanse? That is exactly what the word *Sahara* means in Arabic—"deserts." So vast is that domain that it is not sufficient to speak in the singular. So it is with God, and that is why the ancient Hebrews spoke of Him in the plural.

Third, we are reminded that there is more than meets the eye when we read the scriptures. The English words on the page may seem obvious and apparent to us. Yet often there is more to learn as we faithfully ask probing questions, learn about different translations, and understand the transmission history of the Bible and other scriptures: "We believe the Bible to be the word of God as far as it is translated correctly" (Articles of Faith 1:8).

## Yahweh Is the LORD

Another title for God that appears regularly in the Bible is *LORD* in all capital letters. When you read the Bible and see LORD in all caps, you can immediately know that the translators were reverently representing the name of God: *Yahweh*. Our English word *Jehovah* derives from the Hebrew word *Yahweh*.

*Yahweh* is one of the most significant words in all the Hebrew language. We hear echoes of it when Moses encounters the LORD at the burning bush on Mount Sinai and asks for the name of the God who was commanding him to deliver the Israelites from Egyptian bondage: "Behold, when I come unto the children of Israel, and shall say unto them, The God of your fathers hath sent me unto you; and they shall say to me, What is his name? what shall I say unto them?" (Exodus 3:13).

God responded to Moses, "I AM THAT I AM: and he said, Thus shalt thou say unto the children of Israel, I AM hath sent me unto you" (Exodus 3:14). In a loose translation of the Hebrew, God said to Moses, "My name is *Yahweh*. Tell the Israelites that Yahweh sent you."

The word *Yahweh* is the present tense of the Hebrew verb "to be." Other English translations of *Yahweh*'s name could include "The Self-Existing One," "The Being," or simply "Is."

Significantly, and distinct from many languages I have studied, the present tense of the verb "to be" in Hebrew is reserved wholly and singularly for *Yahweh*. If I want to say in Hebrew, "I am a man," I simply say, "I a man." Readers and listeners will fill in the context of the missing verb "to be" (in this case, the present-tense form "am"). In English, of course, it sounds silly to say phrases without the verb "to be"—consider "She a girl," "That a dog," "He a boy," or "You a friend." Instead, we appropriately expect to hear, "She is a girl," "That is a dog," "He is a boy," or "You are a friend." You'll often notice in our English versions of the Old Testament italicized present-tense forms of the verb "to be"; that's because the words do not appear in the Hebrew, so the translators supplied them for us, indicated by italics in print editions. See for example Genesis 1:29, where the present-tense verb *is* is italicized: "And God said, Behold, I have given you every herb bearing seed, which *is* upon the face of all the earth, and every tree, in the which *is* the fruit of a tree yielding seed; to you it shall be for meat."

Think of the stunning symbolism and awesome reality that an entire language reserves the utterance of any present tense form of "to be" to God Himself, whose name is "The Self-Existing One": *Yahweh*.

The next time you read the scriptures, especially the Old Testament, and see the word *God*, know that in ancient Hebrew this read *Gods*. When you see the word *LORD* in all caps in the Bible, know that the translators reverently did not say the name *Yahweh*. And when you remember that *LORD* = *Yahweh*, you can also remember that He, The Self-Existing One, is the reason that all things *ARE*.

Why do I share all of this in a book dedicated to the Book of Mormon? Because in the chapter titled, "Why One of the Most Common Phrases in the Book of Mormon Is Also the Most Meaningful," I'll discuss one of the most commonly used phrases in the Book of Mormon and why it so significantly connects to the name of God.

# THE SURPRISING MEANINGS OF BOOK OF MORMON NAMES AND HOW THEY WITNESS THAT THE BOOK OF MORMON IS AN AUTHENTIC WITNESS FOR JESUS CHRIST[4]

By Taylor Halverson, PhD, and Brad Wilcox, PhD

ANCIENT SCRIPTURE WRITERS OFTEN USED the literary pattern of *paronomasia* (word plays and word puns) to convey significant theological messages. Old Testament writers used the meanings of names to help people remember the key idea of a story.

When the first man Adam is introduced in Genesis 2:7, the scripture reads, "And the LORD God formed man [*adam*] of the dust of the ground [*adama*]" (emphasis added). Adam's name is related to the Hebrew word *adama*, which means "ground, earth, dirt, or dust." Adam's name reminds us that God created us all from the dust of the earth (*adama*). And just as the dust of the earth (*adama*) obeys the voice of its Maker, so should we.

Look at how the Book of Mormon provides similar meaning: "O how great is the nothingness of the children of men [*adam*]; yea, even they are less than the dust of the earth [*adama*]. For behold, the dust of the earth [*adama*] moveth hither and thither, to the dividing asunder, at the command of our great and everlasting God" (Helaman 12:7–8; emphasis added).

The first woman was Eve. Her Hebrew name means "life." Adam identifies the meaning of her name as a main idea of the story in Genesis 3:20: "And Adam called his wife's name Eve [*havva*]; because she was the mother of all living [*hai*]" (emphasis added). We appropriately honor Eve [*havva*] as the first woman for being the mother of all living [*hai*] children of God.

This Old Testament pattern of using the name of an individual to teach a key idea was continued by Nephi and other Book of Mormon writers—a fact we see as compelling evidence for the authenticity of the Book of Mormon. If we could read the original Hebrew and Egyptian texts of the Book of Mormon, we'd find names repeated thematically throughout the text. Just as modern persuasive writers today repeat their thesis statements in multiple ways throughout their writing, so too ancient prophets used names and derivatives of names to reinforce in meaningful ways the major idea they wished for readers to see in the text. Such wordplays constitute the beautiful, significant, even brilliant literary sophistication of Book of Mormon writers.

Prophets also employed names to call our attention to other individuals in scripture with the same name. Remember when Helaman named his sons Nephi and Lehi (see Helaman 5:6–7)? He did so to call to their remembrance the good lives of their forefathers. But such naming and remembering goes beyond simply thinking of another similarly named person. Naming and wordplay provide opportunities to compare and contrast scripture stories that might otherwise not be brought together.

The meanings of these names can point us to a deeper appreciation for the lives of the real people who are found in the pages of the Book of Mormon, that their lives can guide us to a deeper understanding of Jesus and to the truth that the Book of Mormon is an authentic witness for Jesus.

## Nephi

*Nephi* seems to be an ancient Egyptian name. One word in Egyptian that sounds like Nephi means "sea captain."[5] This would be a fitting meaning for Nephi, since with the Lord's help he built a ship and navigated the seas.

However, *Nephi* is more likely an Egyptian word that means "good, fair, delightful, or beautiful." Nephi's choices made him good and fair. Even when he declared that he was a wretched man, his trust in the Lord was delightful and beautiful.

Helaman named one of his sons after the original Nephi because he was "good." Helaman told his son, "I would that ye should do that which is good" (Helaman 5:7). In the same way, Nephi's name can remind us that we should always try to lead others toward God and seek after all that is good, fair, delightful, and beautiful (see Articles of Faith 1:13).

## Sariah

Sariah, one of the few named women in the Book of Mormon, has a Hebrew name that means "Jehovah is a prince/captain." What do princes or captains do? They command. They protect. They deliver. They empower. Only two direct quotes are attributed to Sariah in the Book of Mormon. In one, she expresses her faith in the princely powers of Jehovah—that is, the powers to command, protect, save, and deliver. When her sons safely return from confronting Laban, her expression of faith plays upon the meaning of her own name and does it in beautiful chiastic structure:

A   "Now I know of a surety that the **Lord** [*iah*] hath **commanded** [*sar*]
    my husband to flee into the wilderness;
    B   yea, and I also know of a surety that the **Lord** [*iah*]
        hath <u>protected</u> my sons,
        and <u>delivered</u> them out of the hands of Laban,
        and given them <u>power</u>
A   whereby they could accomplish the thing which the **Lord** [*iah*]
    hath **commanded** [*sar*] them" (1 Nephi 5:8, emphasis
    added).

Significantly, mother Sariah's testimony seems to have had a powerful impact on Nephi's own testimony, evident in his declaration, "I will go and do the things which the **Lord** [*iah*] hath **commanded** [*sar*], for I know that the **Lord** [*iah*] giveth no **commandments** [*sar*] unto the children of men, save he shall prepare a way for them that they may accomplish the thing which he [Lord/*iah*] **commandeth** [*sar*] them" (1 Nephi 3:7; emphasis added).

Like Sariah, let us choose Jehovah as our prince and commander. Then we will also "endure [our suffering] well, God shall exalt [us] on high; [and we] shalt triumph over all [our] foes" (D&C 121:8) just as Sariah declared Jehovah had empowered her sons to do to their enemies.

## Enos

*Enos* was one of the first words Hebrew children learned. Enos simply means "man." The prophet named Enos in the Book of Mormon was a true man of God. Perhaps his name was meant to remind Enos that the One we worship is the Man of Holiness (see Moses 6:57). These ideas heighten the complexity and meaning of Enos's name. No longer does his name seem simple. Rather, his name invited him and all of us to remember the Man we call Father—to seek to live like Him, emulate Him, and render Him thanks all day and all night.

Enos can also be seen as a wordplay hearkening back to the patriarch Jacob's nighttime wrestle with an angel (see Genesis 32:24–32). Like Jacob from the Old Testament, Enos wrestled before the Lord all night long, seeking answers and seeking blessings. If we peel back the translation of the Bible and look at the Hebrew, we see that the angel who wrestled with Jacob was called an *enos*, a man (see Genesis 32:24). So perhaps the Book of Mormon writers included this story of Enos to teach us that, like the great prophet Enos and the great patriarch Jacob, we too can engage in the wrestle for blessings, faith, and humility. We can have confidence that God will answer our prayers and grant us the righteous blessings we seek.

## Alma

For years, critics of the Book of Mormon claimed that Alma was misused as a male name. After all, the Latin word *alma* is a girl's name and is associated only with feminine virtues. For example, we use the phrase *alma mater* to represent our schools. In Latin, those words mean "nourishing mother."

However, the original language of the Book of Mormon was not Latin but an adaptation of Semitic languages like Egyptian and Hebrew (see Mormon 9:32–33). In Hebrew, *alma* actually means "young man." This helps us remember that both Alma and his son Alma were young men when they were converted and chose to devote their lives to the Lord. In fact, Mormon may have been using some literary devices like alliteration and assonance in the original text—literary devices that were lost in the English translation: "But there was one among them whose name was Alma, he also being a descendant of Nephi. And he was a young man [*alma*], and he believed [*amen*] the words [*emerim*] which Abinadi had spoken [*amar*]" (Mosiah 17:2; emphasis added). The similarity of words would have solidified the meaning of Alma's name in the minds of ancient readers and connected it with other words about faith and gospel teaching.

Knowing the meaning of Alma's name reminds us to seek the Lord early, while in our youth (see "Seek the Lord Early," *Children's Songbook*, 108). Like Alma the Elder and Alma the Younger, we must make the choice to devote our entire lives to God's service.

## Noah

King Noah in the Book of Mormon was such a notorious character. It seems inappropriate that he would carry the same name as the noble prophet Noah from the Old Testament. However, there are lessons to be learned from the name regardless of its bearers.

In Hebrew, *Noah* means "rest." From an Old Testament standpoint, we can immediately see the wordplay in the Genesis stories of Noah (see Genesis 6–9). God wanted to rest from the wickedness of the world, the ark came to rest on Mount Ararat, and the dove could find no rest until the waters dried up.

But what does the name *Noah* mean in the Book of Mormon? Significantly, the word *Noah* can also have the negative meaning of "lazy." And who is the laziest king in the entire Book of Mormon? King Noah! It is easy to see how lazy the king and his priests are when contrasted with the industrious and heavy-laboring citizens:

> Yea, and thus [King Noah and his wicked priests] were supported in their **laziness**, and in their idolatry, and in their whoredoms, by the taxes which king Noah had put upon his people; thus did the people **labor** exceedingly to support iniquity. (Mosiah 11:6; emphasis added)

And:

> The seats which were set apart for the high priests, which were above all the other seats, he did ornament with pure gold; and he caused a breastwork to be built before them, that they might **rest** their bodies and their arms upon while they should speak lying and vain words to his people. (Mosiah 11:11; emphasis added)

The Book of Mormon shows us what happens when a society has a lazy king (like Noah) compared to righteous kings (like Benjamin or Mosiah II) who labored in the service of their people.

Another unexpected insight from this story can be derived by comparing some of the broad outlines of the story of King Noah to Noah in the Bible. In both stories, men called Noah introduced viticulture (the planting of vineyards, winemaking, and drunkenness) into society.

Noah in the Old Testament was the first person mentioned who planted a vineyard and who also later became drunk. King Noah was the first person mentioned in the Book of Mormon to plant vineyards and to bring about drunkenness. Significantly in each story, curses follow drunkenness.

I doubt that the young and relatively uneducated Joseph Smith would have been able to create such a brilliant use of Hebrew wordplay with the name *Noah* in the Book of Mormon. Perhaps he could have thought to use a positive Bible name for a negative character, but it's unlikely that he could have provided a story arc that captured the subtle contours and theological message of Noah in the Old Testament. Not only does this provide authenticity for the veracity of the Book of Mormon, these insights provide additional meaning and beauty to the story of Noah in both the Old Testament and the Book of Mormon.

## Heshlon

In the Book of Ether, we find the name *Heshlon*. Although we aren't completely certain about the meaning of names in the book of Ether (or in the Book of Mormon, for that matter), *Heshlon* appears to mean "the place of crushing" in Hebrew. If we look at where this name appears in the Book of Mormon, we come across some striking insights. Heshlon is the place where destructive and disastrous battles occurred. Many were killed in the back and forth between two great armies.

If we render the relevant passages in chiastic literary form (another ancient Near Eastern literary technique centered on a major idea), we see that the word *Heshlon* is at the very middle of a chiasm. The word literally and literarily demonstrates its own meaning, "the place of crushing," as it is crushed between the competing ends of the chiasmus:

**A** a Now there began to be a war **upon all the face of the land**,
    b **every man**
        c with his <u>band</u>
            d fighting for that which he desired.
        c' And there were <u>robbers</u>,
    b' and in fine, **all** <u>manner of wickedness</u>
a' **upon all the face of the land**.
    B a And it came to pass that Coriantumr was <u>exceedingly angry</u> with Shared,

b and <u>he went against him with his armies to</u> **battle**;
a' and they did meet in <u>great anger</u>,
  b' and they did meet <u>in the **valley of Gilgal**</u>; and <u>the</u> **battle**
a" became <u>exceedingly sore</u>.
  b" And it came to pass that Shared **fought** against him **for the space of three days**.
      C And it came to pass that **Coriantumr beat him**,
          D and did pursue him until he came to **the plains**
              X **of Heshlon**.
          D' And it came to pass that Shared gave him battle again upon <u>the plains</u>;
      C' and behold, he <u>did beat Coriantumr</u>,
  B' and drove him back again to the <u>valley of Gilgal</u>.
      b" And Coriantumr gave Shared <u>battle</u> again in the <u>valley of Gilgal</u>,
          a''' in which he <u>beat</u> Shared and <u>slew him</u>.
          a''' And Shared <u>wounded</u> Coriantumr in his thigh,
      b''' that he did not go to **battle** again **for the space of two years**,
A' b" in which time **all the people**
  a' **upon the face of the land**
          d' were shedding blood,
      b''' and **there was none** to restrain them (Ether 13:25–31; emphasis added).[6]

Not only are the presence of ancient literary structures in the Book of Mormon amazing, but they survived translation into English. That is even more amazing and far beyond the capabilities of young Joseph Smith.

## Mormon

Joseph Smith was once asked the meaning of the word *Mormon*. He responded that it means "more good." Although Joseph did not give the actual Egyptian meaning of the word at that time, he certainly taught everyone that following Mormon would ultimately lead them to Jesus Christ and the "more good" found within the fullness of His restored gospel (see Matthew L. Bowen, "'Most Desirable Above All Things': Onomastic Play on Mary and Mormon in the Book of Mormon," *Interpreter: A Journal of Latter-day Saint Faith and Scholarship 13* [2015]: 27–61).

The meaning of Mormon's name is a combination of two ancient Egyptian words: *mr*, which means "love," and *mn*, which means "enduring" and "everlasting." The two words together mean "love endures forever." Remembering the meaning of Mormon's name can help us remember the prophet who wrote, compiled, and preserved the Book of Mormon and testified that the love of God through Jesus Christ endures forever. It can help us remember that Mormon gave one of the greatest discourses on the pure love of Christ ever recorded: "But charity is the pure love of Christ, and it endureth forever; and whoso is found possessed of it at the last day, it shall be well with him" (Moroni 7:47).

Even though Mormon lived in a corrupt civilization full of degradation and violence, he taught of love and charity for all. We also live in perilous times and find ourselves in challenging circumstances. We should always strive to be "more good," as Joseph Smith suggested, but even when we slip and fall we can have confidence that God's love is perfect and it endures forever. In that love we can find the grace that will enable us to keep trying and never lose hope.

## Moroni

Moroni was the last recorded Nephite. We hear his anguished expressions of loneliness and solitude in the concluding section of the Book of Mormon as he wanders for decades finishing the record abridged by his father, Mormon. Soon after Moroni took over his father's solemn duties as sacred record keeper, he recorded, "**I am alone**. My father hath been slain in battle, and all my kinsfolk, and I have not friends nor whither to go; and how long the Lord will suffer that I may live I know not" (Mormon 8:5; emphasis added).

Hauntingly, Moroni's name sounds like an Egyptian word that means "I was beloved." Think of it! Moroni was beloved by his father, Mormon (whose name means "love endures forever"). Moroni was likely beloved by a wife, children, brothers and sisters, a mother, friends—all of them gone, left "to crumble and to return to their mother earth" (Mormon 6:15). Moroni was entirely alone, except for the voices of those on the plates he carried and the voice of Jesus Christ, who guided him. When we feel alone, we must remind ourselves that we, like Moroni, are beloved.

## Conclusion

The Book of Mormon is literarily beautiful, doctrinally truthful, and everlastingly applicable. These simple names in its pages prove to not be so simple after all. They stand as additional evidence that the book is of ancient origin and was brought forth by the gift and power of God.[7]

# WHY ONE OF THE MOST COMMON PHRASES IN THE BOOK OF MORMON IS ALSO THE MOST MEANINGFUL[8]

MARK TWAIN FAMOUSLY QUIPPED THAT if Joseph Smith had left out the phrase "it came to pass," the Book of Mormon would have been no more than a short pamphlet.[9]

We may justifiably join Mark Twain in wondering why the phrase "it came to pass" is used in the Book of Mormon *ad nauseum* (a fancy phrase that means "until we are literally sick!"). It's like listening to high school teenagers, who use the word *like* about every third word and, like, no one even knows why.

Joking aside, why does this phrase show up so often? Let me suggest several reasons that I hope expand our love, gratitude, and understanding of scripture and God's character.

## The Comforting Message of "It Came to Pass"

This first insight is more of a personal opinion, but I feel a deep sense of perspective when I consider the literal meaning of the phrase "it came to pass." Read that again and think specifically about what it means. *Nothing in this mortal life comes to stay.* I find that truth deeply heartening because life is so full of pain, anguish, worry, and heartache.

Sure, I know we all signed up for this, and somewhere in the Old Testament, we are told that we shouted for joy about all the pain and suffering we'd experience in this life. I say that tongue-in-cheek, of course, because without pain and suffering we could never know the joy of salvation—that sweet fruit of redemption that comes through Jesus Christ and that is so beautifully declared by mother Eve: "Were it not for our transgression we never should have had seed, and never should have known good and evil, and the joy of our redemption, and the eternal life which God giveth unto all the obedient" (Moses 5:11).

But consider again the liberating truth of the phrase, "it came to pass." Remember: We are here to be tried and tested. And if we endure it well, we will be exalted on high (see D&C 121:8). No pain, no loss, no heartache, no grief, no shattered dream will be your permanent reality. Those things come. Then they pass on by.

Like Mother Eve or faithful Joseph Smith, we can learn to endure well as we remember,

> know thou, my son, that all these things shall give thee experience, and shall be for thy good.
>
> The Son of Man hath descended below them all. Art thou greater than he?
>
> Therefore, hold on thy way, and the priesthood shall remain with thee; for their bounds are set, they cannot pass. Thy days are known, and thy years shall not be numbered less; therefore, fear not what man can do, for God shall be with you forever and ever. (D&C 122:7–9)

## Literary Insights

We all know that an engine is what propels and drives a car forward. The thrill of speed is initiated every time the engine is kicked into gear. Conversely, if there's no engine, there's no movement.

Similar to the engine of a car, the phrase "it came to pass" is an ancient Hebrew literary convention that helped a narrative have energy, flow, and dynamism.

In modern English, we might tell a story without verbally marking the onward, driving force of the narrative: I woke up this morning. I ate breakfast. I drove to work. I came home. And I went to bed.

That isn't a very compelling story (perhaps a bit too close to home for lovers of the movie *Groundhog Day*). Furthermore, it doesn't let us feel the energy of flowing narrative. We aren't carried along effortlessly point by point. Rather, each statement is a staccato experience that speaks a single truth but not in a connected, engaging fashion.

To avoid such stifling narrative expressions, ancient Hebrew writers liberally spread the phrase "it came to pass" throughout their narratives. The reader would feel the movement and acceleration of the narrative; there was no time to pause on any one action, because it was time to pick up and move on to the next action or idea. There is purpose and excitement in the text. There is a story to be told and no time to lose by dwelling on a particular scene.

Perhaps I can try one more analogy. Modern action movies are made up of quick action scenes with hurried editorial cuts. Just watch the latest action blockbuster, and during a particularly energetic action scene, count how many visual transitions occur in a single minute. A particularly fast-paced movie may have thirty or more visual transitions in *a single minute.* That's one transition every two seconds. Why do movie makers do that? Because it creates a heightened sense of movement, of story flow, of energy, of engagingly interconnected narrative building blocks that have been brought together seamlessly so the story flows breathlessly and satisfyingly from one moment to the next.

That's exactly how the phrase "it came to pass" functioned in ancient Hebrew writing.

As highly capable and trained scribes, Nephi and other Book of Mormon writers did not want to keep their readers stuck in the doldrums of unconnected narrative building blocks. They wanted to punch the gas pedal of the narrative and use the engine of "it came to pass" to drive the flow and development and energy of the story forward.

This final insight may be the most striking reason why "it came to pass" is one of the most significant phrases in all the scriptures.

In Hebrew, the phrase "it came to pass" is built on the same Hebrew root word for the personal name of God: *Yahweh.* As indicated in an earlier chapter, the word *Yahweh* is the present tense of the Hebrew verb "to be." Other English translations of Yahweh's name could include "The Self-Existing One," "The Being," or simply "Is." Significantly, and distinct from many languages that I have studied, the present tense of the verb "to be" in Hebrew is reserved wholly and singularly for *Yahweh.* Think of the stunning symbolism and awesome reality that an entire language reserves the utterance of any present-tense form of "to be" to God Himself, whose name is "The Self-Existing One"—*Yahweh.*

How does this relate to the phrase "it came to pass" in the Book of Mormon?

Since the phrase "it came to pass" is built on the same root word for the name of God—*Yahweh,* who is The Self-Existing One, who makes all that is—then the insight is that Yahweh is the source and the cause that brings everything into existence, who drives the narrative of the plan of salvation, the narrative of our very lives, forward to completion. As the one who "IS," who brings to pass all things, He is the Author and Finisher of our faith.

When we read "it came to pass," we see God's presence, His love, His concern, His energy, His knowledge, His direction, His guidance.

Truly, God, as *Yahweh*, is the One who makes all that is and brings to pass all that is necessary for our eternal salvation.

## Conclusion

Rather than the repetitive, pedestrian phrase that seems to do no more than clutter the Book of Mormon, "it came to pass" may be one of the most significant, meaningful, and overlooked phrases of the entire Book of Mormon. With this understanding, perhaps we can be at peace to let God bring to pass His great and marvelous work in our own lives and throughout His created order.

# WHAT DOES GOD EXPECT OF KINGS? INSIGHTS FROM DEUTERONOMY 17 APPLIED TO THE BOOK OF MORMON[10]

LIKELY THE MOST SUCCINCT SET of verses in the Bible that expresses God's expectation for a king[11] are found in Deuteronomy 17:14–20.[12] These verses, I argue, are crucial criteria for understanding Book of Mormon kingship.[13]

When thou art come unto the land which the LORD thy God giveth thee, and shalt possess it, and shalt dwell therein, and shalt say, I will set a king over me, like as all the nations that are about me;

Thou shalt in any wise set him king over thee, whom the LORD thy God shall choose: one from among thy brethren shalt thou set king over thee: thou mayest not set a stranger over thee, which is not thy brother.

But he shall not multiply horses to himself, nor cause the people to return to Egypt, to the end that he should multiply horses: forasmuch as the LORD hath said unto you, Ye shall henceforth return no more that way.

Neither shall he multiply wives to himself, that his heart turn not away: neither shall he greatly multiply to himself silver and gold.

And it shall be, when he sitteth upon the throne of his kingdom, that he shall write him a copy of this law in a book out of that which is before the priests the Levites:

And it shall be with him, and he shall read therein all the days of his life: that he may learn to fear the LORD his God, to keep all the words of this law and these statutes, to do them:

That his heart be not lifted up above his brethren, and
that he turn not aside from the commandment, to the right
hand, or to the left: to the end that he may prolong his
days in his kingdom, he, and his children, in the midst of
Israel.

I interpret these passages as a set of God-decreed kingly dos and don'ts.
I'll begin with the don'ts:

1. Don't acquire many horses—in other words, don't raise a military
   (v. 16).
2. Don't return the people to Egypt—in other words, don't return
   people to the house of bondage/apostasy (v. 16).
3. Don't acquire many wives (v. 17).[14]
4. Don't seek after silver and gold (v. 17).
5. Don't lift yourself up above your brethren (v. 20).

What *should* the king be doing with all his time and influence?

1. Have a copy of the scriptures (v. 18).
2. Read the scriptures every day (v. 18).
3. Teach the scriptures (vv. 19–20).

Remarkably, God doesn't want a human king to do *any* of the things
we typically associate with leaders. Rather, God simply wants a leader who
is a lover of scripture. Why? Because God Himself is the king. As Jacob so
beautiful records, "For he that raiseth up a king against me shall perish, *for
I, the Lord, the king of heaven, will be their king*, and I will be a light unto
them forever, that hear my words" (2 Nephi 10:14; emphasis added).

There is no need to replace God on the divine throne of kingship with
some fallible human king. Unfortunately, humans have managed to usurp
God's role and power as king in a masterful way.

The Book of Mormon narrative is driven, in part, by this very pressing
question: "Who is to be the king?" How that question was asked and
answered contributed to significant portions of Book of Mormon narrative
production.[15]

What is so striking about the seven verses quoted earlier from
Deuteronomy is that expressions of Book of Mormon kingship align
so well with this rubric for kingship. For those who seek to argue that

Joseph Smith was the imaginative and enterprising author of the Book of Mormon, I find it difficult to believe that Joseph Smith was so versed in the Bible that he could correctly identify *the only seven consecutive verses in the entire Bible where God lays out His dos and don'ts for kingship* and then build a book of hundreds of thousands of words that contains kingship narratives that seem to be strong examples and counterexamples of what happens when kings do or do not fulfill God's expectations.

Here are some compelling examples of how well the Book of Mormon represents God's expectations for kingship as set forth in Deuteronomy 17.[16]

### Nephi Evaluated Against Deuteronomy 17

| Don't | How did Nephi do? Exemplary king |
|---|---|
| Deuteronomy 17:16 *Don't acquire many horses (don't raise a military).* | 2 Nephi 5:14; 2 Nephi 4:34 *There is no mention of Nephi seeking after horses, though he did arm his people to defend themselves from enemies. But his trust was not in the arm of flesh but in the Lord.* |
| Deuteronomy 17:16 *Don't return the people to Egypt (don't return people to the house of bondage/apostasy).* | 1 Nephi 18:22 *Nephi led the people into a new promised land, just as Moses did.* |
| Deuteronomy 17:17 *Don't acquire many wives.* | 1 Nephi 16:7 *Nephi did not seek after additional wives.* |
| Deuteronomy 17:17 *Don't seek after silver and gold.* | 1 Nephi 18:25 *Nephi did seek after silver and gold but only with the intent to support his society, not to empower or ingratiate himself.* |

| Deuteronomy 17:20 *Don't lift yourself up above your brethren.* | 1 Nephi 17:55; 2 Nephi 5:19–20 *Nephi did not lift himself up above his people. In fact, he rejected the title of king.* |
|---|---|
| **Do** | **How did Nephi do? Exemplary king** |
| Deuteronomy 17:18 *Have a copy of the scriptures.* | 1 Nephi 3:24 *Nephi obtained the scriptures from Laban.* |
| Deuteronomy 17:19 *Read the scriptures every day.* | 2 Nephi 25:26 *Nephi was quite passionate about the scriptures, so likely he was a regular reader.* |
| Deuteronomy 17:19 *Live and teach the scriptures.* | 1 Nephi 19:23–24 *Nephi lived and taught the scriptures.* |

In summary, Nephi fulfilled God's expectations of kingship in an exemplary fashion.

### Benjamin Evaluated Against Deuteronomy 17

| **Don't** | **How did Benjamin do? Exemplary king** |
|---|---|
| Deuteronomy 17:16 *Don't acquire many horses (don't raise a military).* | Words of Mormon 13–14 *King Benjamin protected his people from enemies and apparently had a military, but they fought their enemies in the strength of the Lord.* |
| Deuteronomy 17:16 *Don't return the people to Egypt (don't return people to the house of bondage/apostasy).* | Words of Mormon 15–18 *King Benjamin did not lead people to apostasy.* |

| Deuteronomy 17:17 *Don't acquire many wives.* | *King Benjamin did not seek after additional wives.* [There are no scriptures indicating that King Benjamin sought additional wives.] |
| --- | --- |
| Deuteronomy 17:17 *Don't seek after silver and gold.* | Mosiah 2:12, 14 *King Benjamin did not seek after the wealth of the world.* |
| Deuteronomy 17:20 *Don't lift yourself up above your brethren.* | Mosiah 2:10–11 *King Benjamin did not lift himself up above his people.* |
| **Do** | **How did Benjamin do? Exemplary king** |
| Deuteronomy 17:18 *Have a copy of the scriptures.* | Mosiah 1:2–3 *King Benjamin had the scriptures.* |
| Deuteronomy 17:19 *Read the scriptures every day.* | *Likely.* [There is no specific scripture indicating that King Benjamin read the scriptures daily. However, the thrust of this prescription in Deuteronomy is that the king should be a scriptorian. King Benjamin, according to the Book of Mormon record, appears to have thoroughly immersed his life in the scriptures.] |
| Deuteronomy 17:19 *Live and teach the scriptures.* | Mosiah 1:2–3; 2:9–11 *King Benjamin lived and taught the scriptures to his sons and to his people.* |

Like Nephi, Benjamin fulfilled God's expectations of kingship in an exemplary fashion.

## King Noah Evaluated Against Deuteronomy 17

| Don't | How did Noah do? Disastrous king |
|---|---|
| Deuteronomy 17:16 *Don't acquire many horses (don't raise a military).[17]* | Mosiah 11:18–19 *Noah raised a military; he put his trust in the arm of flesh instead of in God, who is the divine warrior!* |
| Deuteronomy 17:16 *Don't return the people to Egypt (don't return people to the house of bondage/apostasy).* | Mosiah 11:2; 19:28; 21:3–5 *Noah led the people into apostasy and bondage.* |
| Deuteronomy 17:17 *Don't acquire many wives.* | Mosiah 11:2 *Noah had many wives and concubines.* |
| Deuteronomy 17:17 *Don't seek after silver and gold.* | Mosiah 11:3–4 *Noah sought the gold and silver of the people for his own purposes.* |
| Deuteronomy 17:20 *Don't lift yourself up above your brethren.* | Mosiah 11:9–12; 19:6–11 *Noah lifted himself up above the people.* |
| **Do** | **How did Noah do? Disastrous king** |
| Deuteronomy 17:18 *Have a copy of the scriptures.* | Mosiah 11:27, 29 *Noah was apparently ignorant of scriptures.* |
| Deuteronomy 17:19 *Read the scriptures every day.* | *Noah gave that role to the priests.* [No scripture indicates that Noah had any awareness of scripture. Instead, the priests are the primary agitators in the trial of Abinadi, misusing scripture in an attempt to trap Abinadi.] |

| Deuteronomy 17:19 *Live and teach the scriptures.* | *No.* [Noah did not live or teach the scriptures. In fact, the priests, to whom he delegated his role as scriptorian, appear to be familiar with scripture, but they misuse scripture in an attempt to destroy Abinadi.] |
|---|---|

King Noah was a spectacular failure in living as God expected kings to live. In fact, it is striking how distinctly opposite all Noah's actions were from God's ideal for kingship as set forth in Deuteronomy 17:14–20.

## Mosiah II Evaluated Against Deuteronomy 17

| Don't | How did Mosiah II do? Exemplary king |
|---|---|
| Deuteronomy 17:16 *Don't acquire many horses (don't raise a military).* | Mosiah 29:14 *Mosiah II protected his people from enemies; while he may have had a military, but his trust was not in the arm of flesh but in the Lord.* |
| Deuteronomy 17:16 *Don't return the people to Egypt (don't return people to the house of bondage/apostasy).* | Mosiah 29:33–37 *Mosiah II did not lead people to apostasy.* |
| Deuteronomy 17:17 *Don't acquire many wives.* | *Mosiah II did not seek after additional wives.* [There are no scriptures indicating that Mosiah II had or sought for additional wives.] |
| Deuteronomy 17:17 *Don't seek after silver and gold.* | Mosiah 27:2–5 *Mosiah II did not seek after the wealth of the world.* |

| Deuteronomy 17:20 *Do not lift yourself up above your brethren.* | Mosiah 29: 32, 40 *Mosiah II did not lift himself up above his people.* |
|---|---|
| **Do** | **How did Mosiah II do? Exemplary king** |
| Deuteronomy 17:18 *Have a copy of the scriptures.* | Mosiah 28:11, 17 *Mosiah II had the scriptures. It was the writings/scriptures that likely helped convince him to get rid of kingship.* |
| Deuteronomy 17:19 *Read the scriptures every day.* | Mosiah 28:10–13 *Mosiah II likely read the scriptures often.* |
| Deuteronomy 17:19 *Live and teach the scriptures.* | Mosiah 25:4–7, 14; 28:14, 17–18 *Mosiah II lived and taught the scriptures to his sons and to his people.* |

Like Nephi and Benjamin, Mosiah II fulfilled God's expectations of kingship in an exemplary fashion.

I believe that the Book of Mosiah was constructed as a sandwich narrative: good king [Benjamin], then bad king [Noah], then good king [Mosiah II]. This narrative structure highlights why Mosiah II recognized the problem of kingship. Kingship was a major factor in Nephite conflict, suffering, and apostasy. Mosiah II therefore was motivated to disband kingship. Ironically, much of the historical backdrop for the book of Alma and the book of Helaman revolves around people fighting for a return to kingship while others fight to avoid kingship.

## Conclusion

If Joseph Smith was the presumed author of the Book of Mormon, it is incredibly remarkable that he had enough foresight to construct kingship narratives that so unfailingly adhered to or perfectly disagreed with what God expected of a king as expressed in Deuteronomy 17:14–20. Future studies could take each leader from the Book of Mormon and hold them up to the standard of Deuteronomy 17:14–20. The comparisons and contrasts among Book of Mormon leaders as to how well they fulfilled God's expectations of leaders will likely prove enlightening.[18]

# NEPHI THE SCRIBE[19]

READERS OF THE BOOK OF MORMON often take for granted that it was written at all. In our modern age where literacy rates are high, it is almost inconceivable to imagine a society where perhaps a mere 10 percent of the population are literate (such as was the case in ancient Israel).

It is therefore stunning that Nephi was not only capable of reading and writing, he also was a brilliantly competent writer who created some of the finest literary beauty and artistry that the world has ever known.

The fact that Nephi was literate might initially seem improbable in ancient Israel, where many people lived hand to mouth, eking out a subsistence lifestyle based on what they could farm or herd. Reading and writing was a luxury. What would be the purpose of literacy? So that one could enjoy fine literary pursuits as a pastime after a long day of work? Unlikely.

Why, then, did Nephi know how to read and write?

Being a scribe was an entirely viable profession for the youngest son in a wealthy or elite family. For example, one of the great Neo-Assyrian kings, Ashurbanipal (668 BC to 627 BC), himself the youngest son and therefore least likely to inherit the throne, was trained in the scribal arts of writing, reading, and other educational pursuits. In fact, Ashurbanipal was so capable in and fond of beautiful and important literature that once he became king of the Assyrian Empire, he assembled one of the greatest libraries in the ancient world, the library of Nineveh. A significant portion of what we know of the ancient Middle East is due to Ashurbanipal's literary preservation effort.

Similarly, without Nephi's literary and cultural training, the words we so deeply appreciate in the Book of Mormon would likely never have been written.

Exactly what did it mean to be a scribe? Scribes often practiced their craft by impressing characters on wet clay with a reed stylus. Alternatively, they might have used a form of ink to compose their texts on papyrus. (Incidentally, our modern word *paper* derives from the word *papyrus*.) As they practiced writing, Israelite scribes typically were taught and fully immersed in the principles found in the ancient Wisdom tradition, copying passages from wisdom literature as a way to learn not only the language but also the moral and cultural values. The Old Testament book of Proverbs is a good example of the types of wisdom principles scribes would be expected to write, copy, know, and live.

One piece of evidence in favor of Nephi's training as a scribe in the ancient Near Eastern Wisdom tradition is this: Nephi says that he writes his record with "knowledge" (1 Nephi 1:3). In Hebrew, the word *knowledge* is expressed as *daat*. This is a key word in the wisdom literature section of the Old Testament (Proverbs, Job, Ecclesiastes, Song of Solomon). There are some eighty-nine occurrences of *daat* in the entirety of the Old Testament, and about 70 percent of these occur in the wisdom literature section. Nephi's claim to draw upon "knowledge" may be influenced by his scribal training in the wisdom literature tradition.

Another brilliant but subtle example of Nephi's training as a scribe occurs when Nephi was building the boat. His brothers refused to help, and instead they threatened to harm Nephi. In commanding faith, Nephi declared:

> In the name of the Almighty God, I command you that
> ye touch me not, for I am filled with the power of God, even
> unto the consuming of my flesh; and whoso shall lay his
> hands upon me shall wither *even as a dried reed*; and he shall
> be as naught before the power of God, for God shall smite
> him. (1 Nephi 17:48; emphasis added)

Nephi would know of dry reeds, since they were used to inscribe tablets. Even more compelling and potentially significant is this: In the ancient Near Eastern wisdom literature, humans were poetically identified with cane reeds that wither, fall, and die. As a trained scribe who may have had familiarity with such ancient Near Eastern scribal poetic expressions, Nephi could not have found a more striking, poetic, and ultimately contextually appropriate metaphor for what would happen to his brothers if they touched him.

As intriguing as these details are, perhaps the most important question to ask is this: Why did Nephi write?

Nephi himself answers that question: "For we labor diligently to write, to persuade our children, and also our brethren, to believe in Christ, and to be reconciled to God; for we know that it is by grace that we are saved, after all we can do" (2 Nephi 25:23).

If Nephi was in fact a scribe, he used his professional training to bless the lives of millions.[20]

# READING 1 NEPHI WITH WISDOM[21]

As he opens his account, Nephi states that his record is founded on the learning of the Jews:

> Yea, I make a record in the language of my father, *which consists of the learning of the Jews* and the language of the Egyptians.
>
> And I know that the record which I make is true; and I make it with mine own hand; and I make it according to my knowledge. (1 Nephi 1:2–3; emphasis added)

And what might the learning of the Jews be? To answer that, let's explore the ancient Near Eastern scribal Wisdom tradition[22] and its related literature and themes as a potential backdrop for Nephi's scribal skills, literary capabilities, and thematic outlook.

When interpreting the phrase "learning of the Jews," scholars of the Book of Mormon typically focus on either Nephi's writing ability or on his formal training[23] in some type of ancient Israelite educational system.[24] Given his writing abilities, it seems that Nephi received training as a scribe,[25] a viable and worthy professional occupation for a fourth son with few prospects for receiving the family inheritance.[26] Ancient Near Eastern scribal schools trained students both in practical arts (the skill of reading and writing) as well as in cultural values, typically expressed through pithy, proverbial statements that students repeatedly copied as writing exercises.[27] That is to say, scribes who were trained in reading and writing were fully immersed in the preserved texts of the Wisdom tradition.[28] To be a scribe was at the very least to have intellectually mastered the Wisdom tradition and, more likely, have come to accept, live, and espouse the principles and ideas of the Wisdom tradition.

For Nephi, the learning of the Jews may also have meant a mastery of Hebraic learning that included chiasmus[29] and other scribal literary devices such as paronomasia (word-play and punning),[30] whether expressed in Egyptian or Hebrew characters or a mixture of those languages and scripts.[31] Accordingly, one intriguing possibility is that the learning of the Jews constituted the principles and themes expressed in the ancient Israelite sapiential or Wisdom tradition.[32] This tradition was passed down from a father or a king to a son or a prince or from a scribal teacher to a new scribe.[33] Thus Nephi's scribal training would make him competent in the ancient Israelite Wisdom tradition.

Another connection between Nephi's record and the Old Testament[34] Wisdom tradition is Nephi's assertion that he has drawn upon "knowledge" in making his record (1 Nephi 1:3). The word *knowledge*, or *daat* in Hebrew, is tied up in the Wisdom tradition. In fact, of the eightynine instances of *daat* in the Old Testament, sixty-one are found in Wisdom literature—nearly 70 percent of the total instances of this word in the Old Testament. And of that total, thirty-nine of eighty-nine are found in the book of Proverbs, constituting 44 percent of the overall total usages of the word *daat* in the Old Testament.[35]

While Nephi upholds the *learning* of the Jews, which may be represented by the Wisdom tradition, he rejects the *manner* of the Jews, perhaps represented by their culture and behaviors: "For I, Nephi, have not taught them many things concerning the manner of the Jews; for their works were works of darkness, and their doings were doings of abominations" (2 Nephi 25:2).

If Nephi is influenced by the Wisdom tradition, then reading 1 Nephi 1:2–3[36]—indeed, reading all of Nephi's writings—through the lens of ancient Near Eastern Wisdom literature may open the records of the Book of Mormon in new and fruitful ways.[37] This chapter discusses five ways in which Nephi's writing may reflect the wider Wisdom literature tradition and thus may be a lens for understanding what Nephi meant by *learning of the Jews*.

Nephi reflects the wider Wisdom literature tradition by:

1. Listening to and recording the words of his wise father.
2. Valuing learning and education.

3.  Embracing hard work.
4.  Seeking understanding from the Lord despite suffering and trials.
5.  Demonstrating the difference between the wise man and the fool.

## The Wisdom Tradition Advocates Listening to and Recording the Words of a Wise Father

Proverbs, a representative repository of Wisdom literature in the Old Testament, advocates that a wise son cherish the words of the father:

> My son, keep my words, and lay up my commandments with thee.
> Keep my commandments, and live; and my law as the apple of thine eye.
> Bind them upon thy fingers, write them upon the table of thine heart. (Proverbs 7:1–3)

Nephi's record begins with what may be a declaration of his upbringing in the Wisdom tradition and his authenticity and reliability as a wise son and scribe:

> Yea, I make a record in the language of my father, which consists of the learning of the Jews and the language of the Egyptians.
> And I know that the record which I make is true; and I make it with mine own hand; and I make it according to my knowledge. (1 Nephi 1:2–3)

Nephi appears to be the prototypical wise son of the Wisdom tradition, and he focuses much of his writing on preserving the words of his father, Lehi—the wise father, leader, or king:

> But I shall make an account of my proceedings in my days. Behold, I make an abridgment of the record of my father, upon plates which I have made with mine own hands; wherefore, after I have abridged the record of my father then will I make an account of mine own life. (1 Nephi 1:17)

That Nephi's original record consisted of the book of Lehi demonstrates how deeply Nephi imbibed the sapiential tradition that advocates that the wise son hear the words of his father, preserve those words, and share those words with others:

> My son, if thou wilt receive my words, and hide my commandments with thee;
> So that thou incline thine ear unto wisdom, and apply thine heart to understanding;
> Yea, if thou criest after knowledge, and liftest up thy voice for understanding;
> If thou seekest her as silver, and searchest for her as for hid treasures;
> Then shalt thou understand the fear of the LORD, and find the knowledge of God.
> For the LORD giveth wisdom: out of his mouth cometh knowledge and understanding. (Proverbs 2:1–6)

Nephi fulfilled these proverbial expectations in several ways. First, as he explained, "having great desires to know of the mysteries of God, wherefore, I did cry unto the Lord; and behold he did visit me, and did soften my heart that I did believe all the words which had been spoken by my father" (1 Nephi 2:16). Furthermore, Nephi sought to preserve and transmit the wisdom of his father across the generations:

> And we had obtained the records which the Lord had commanded us, and searched them and found that they were desirable; yea, even of great worth unto us, insomuch that we could preserve the commandments of the Lord unto our children.
> Wherefore, it was wisdom in the Lord that we should carry them with us, as we journeyed in the wilderness towards the land of promise. (1 Nephi 5:21–22)

The fact that the Book of Mormon is with us today is, in part, a fulfillment of the Wisdom tradition to preserve the sayings of the wise:

> Wherefore, the things which are pleasing unto the world
> I do not write, but the things which are pleasing unto God
> and unto those who are not of the world.
>
> Wherefore, I shall give commandment unto my seed,
> that they shall not occupy these plates with things which
> are not of worth unto the children of men. (1 Nephi 6:5–6)

## The Wisdom Tradition Values Learning and Education

The opening statement of the book of Proverbs declares that to be wise is "To know wisdom and instruction; to perceive the words of understanding" (Proverbs 1:2). Nephi states that he makes the record "according to [his] knowledge" (1 Nephi 1:3). This aligns with the thesis in Proverbs that "the fear [in other words, trust in and respect] of the LORD is the beginning of knowledge" (Proverbs 1:7; 9:10).

Soon after Lehi's vision, departure from Jerusalem, and wise counsel to Laman and Lemuel, these older brothers rejected the words of their father, labeling them "foolish imaginations" (1 Nephi 2:11). Nephi, on the other hand, sought after learning and knowledge:

> And it came to pass that I, Nephi, being exceedingly
> young, nevertheless being large in stature, and also having
> great desires to know of the mysteries of God, wherefore, I
> did cry unto the Lord; and behold he did visit me, and did
> soften my heart that I did believe all the words which had
> been spoken by my father; wherefore, I did not rebel against
> him like unto my brothers.
>
> And I spake unto Sam, making known unto him the
> things which the Lord had manifested unto me by his Holy
> Spirit. And it came to pass that he believed in my words.
> (1 Nephi 2:16–17)

Nephi understood the value of the education and learning that written records could provide. It was this logic, including a reference to wisdom, that Nephi used as he attempted to encourage his brothers to return to Laban a second time to request the brass plates:

> And behold, it is *wisdom* in God that we should obtain these records, that we may preserve unto our children the language of our fathers;
>
> And also that we may preserve unto them the words which have been spoken by the mouth of all the holy prophets, which have been delivered unto them by the Spirit and power of God, since the world began, even down unto this present time.
>
> And it came to pass that after this manner of language did I persuade my brethren, that they might be faithful in keeping the commandments of God. (1 Nephi 3:19–20; emphasis added)

Without the records of the wise, learning and wisdom would wither, and the potential for a righteous civilization would be jeopardized.

> Behold the Lord slayeth the wicked to bring forth his righteous purposes. It is better that one man should perish than that a nation should dwindle and perish in unbelief.
>
> And now, when I, Nephi, had heard these words, I remembered the words of the Lord which he spake unto me in the wilderness, saying that: Inasmuch as thy seed shall keep my commandments, they shall prosper in the land of promise.
>
> Yea, and I also thought that they could not keep the commandments of the Lord according to the law of Moses, save they should have the law.
>
> And I also knew that the law was engraven upon the plates of brass.
>
> And again, I knew that the Lord had delivered Laban into my hands for this cause—that I might obtain the records according to his commandments. (1 Nephi 4:13–17)

## The Wisdom Tradition Teaches Hard Work

Similarly, just as the wise should labor to learn, they should also find benefit in hard work and avoid idle talk, for "in all toil there is profit: but mere talk leads only to poverty" (Proverbs 14:23, New Revised Standard Version).

We see this in the Book of Mormon when Nephi immediately engages in the seemingly impossible and arduous task of building a boat:

> And it came to pass that the Lord spake unto me, saying: Thou shalt construct a ship, after the manner which I shall show thee, that I may carry thy people across these waters.
>
> And I said: Lord, whither shall I go that I may find ore to molten, that I may make tools to construct the ship after the manner which thou hast shown unto me?
>
> And it came to pass that the Lord told me whither I should go to find ore, that I might make tools.
>
> And it came to pass that I, Nephi, did make a bellows wherewith to blow the fire, of the skins of beasts; and after I had made a bellows, that I might have wherewith to blow the fire, I did smite two stones together that I might make fire. (1 Nephi 17:8–11)

Even though Nephi is willing to labor with all his might, lazy Laman and Lemuel taunt Nephi for his lack of wisdom (judgment); they speak of Lehi and Nephi, the wise men in the family, as *fools*:

> And now it came to pass that I, Nephi, was exceedingly sorrowful because of the hardness of their hearts; and now when they saw that I began to be sorrowful they were glad in their hearts, insomuch that they did rejoice over me, saying: We knew that ye could not construct a ship, for we knew that ye were lacking in judgment; wherefore, thou canst not accomplish so great a work.
>
> And thou art like unto our father, led away by the foolish imaginations of his heart; yea, he hath led us out of the land of Jerusalem, and we have wandered in the wilderness for these many years; and our women have toiled, being big with child; and they have borne children in the wilderness and suffered all things, save it were death; and it would have been better that they had died before they came out of Jerusalem than to have suffered these afflictions.

> Behold, these many years we have suffered in the wilderness, which time we might have enjoyed our possessions and the land of our inheritance; yea, and we might have been happy. (1 Nephi 17:19–21)

The Wisdom tradition typically concluded that the righteous prosper and are happy; the wicked are fools who suffer. In that light, Nephi repeats Wisdom-tradition-influenced statements to his brothers, saying that "he that is righteous is favored of God" (1 Nephi 17:35). Considering the difficulties and suffering of the journey, Laman and Lemuel might have felt justified in calling Nephi and Lehi fools who lacked judgment.

But just as Proverb describes "the talk of the lips *tendeth* only to penury" (Proverbs 14:23), Laman and Lemuel's foolish words and threats nearly brought down God's wrath:

> In the name of the Almighty God, I command you that ye touch me not, for I am filled with the power of God, even unto the consuming of my flesh; and whoso shall lay his hands upon me shall wither even as a dried reed; and he shall be as naught before the power of God, for God shall smite him. (1 Nephi 17:48)

As mentioned in the previous chapter, Nephi's reference to "a dried reed" likely came from his experience in the scribal tradition where clay tablets were inscribed using dry reeds. Significantly, cane reeds were often equated with humans in Mesopotamian Wisdom literature. For example, just as a cane reed will eventually fall and die, so too will humans.[38] Once again, Nephi appears to be invoking contextually appropriate themes from the ancient Near Eastern Wisdom tradition to address his circumstances.

## The Wisdom Tradition Instructs One to Seek Knowledge from the Lord Despite Suffering

Like other prominent figures in Wisdom literature, Nephi seeks knowledge from the Lord despite the suffering he personally experiences. Indeed, Nephi describes himself as "having seen many afflictions in the course of [his] days" (1 Nephi 1:1). Like righteous Job, Nephi declares that notwithstanding his trials he still trusts (in other words, fears)[39] the Lord. Thereby, Nephi considers himself "highly favored of the Lord in all [his] days" (1 Nephi 1:1) and affirms that his afflictions led him to gain "a great knowledge of the goodness and the mysteries of God" (1 Nephi 1:1). That sentiment is similar to what Job felt and expressed:

> For I know that my redeemer liveth, and that he shall stand at the latter day upon the earth:
> And though after my skin worms destroy this body, yet in my flesh shall I see God:
> Whom I shall see for myself, and mine eyes shall behold, and not another; though my reins be consumed within me. (Job 19:25–27)

This knowledge leads Nephi to trust in (fear) the Lord, a trust summarized in 1 Nephi 1:20 that likely serves as a thesis statement for the rest of 1 Nephi:

> I, Nephi, will show unto you that the tender mercies of the Lord are over all those whom he hath chosen, because of their faith, to make them mighty even unto the power of deliverance.[40]

### The Wisdom Tradition Clarifies the Difference Between the Wise Man and the Fool

Proverbs contrasts the wise man with the fool: "A wise son maketh a glad father: but a foolish son is the heaviness of his mother" (Proverbs 10:1). Nephi's record provides characters that align with that proverbial contrast. Immediately obvious are Laman and Lemuel, who never truly "hear" the wise words of their father. In the Book of Mormon, they play the role of the fool,[41] the foil to the wise Nephi. Unfortunately, the rebellious brothers may have enacted, or attempted to enact, the seven abominations listed in Proverbs 6:16–19:

> These six things doth the Lord hate: yea, seven are an abomination unto him:
> A proud look, a lying tongue, and hands that shed innocent blood,

An heart that deviseth wicked imaginations, feet that be swift in running to mischief,

A false witness that speaketh lies, and he that soweth discord among brethren.

Another foolish figure in Nephi's record who beautifully plays into the sapiential (wisdom) drama expected of Wisdom literature is Laban. Likely by literary and paronomastic design, Laban's name is an anagram of the Hebrew word *nabal*,[42] meaning "fool."[43] Like a true fool, Laban despises the word of God and fails to value the brass plates in his possession, a direct contrast to Nephi:

Happy is the man that findeth wisdom, and the man that getteth understanding.

For the merchandise of it is better than the merchandise of silver, and the gain thereof than fine gold.

She is more precious than rubies: and all the things thou canst desire are not to be compared unto her. (Proverbs 3:13–15)

Like a fool who lusts for spoil, Laban seeks the property of Nephi's family even though "the getting of treasures by a lying tongue is a vanity tossed to and fro of them that seek death" (Proverbs 21:6). In contrast, wise Nephi is willing to give away his most "valuable" earthly possessions in order to gain the pearl of great price—the wise sayings of the Lord and His prophets as recorded on the brass plates.

A foolish man utters nonsense or speaks without thinking—with dire consequences for himself: "Rash words are like sword thrusts, but the tongue of the wise brings healing" (Proverbs 12:18, New Revised Standard Version; see also Proverbs 6:12–15). Laban is the thoughtless fool when he bears false witness against Laman, saying, "Thou art a robber, and I will slay thee" (1 Nephi 3:13). Significantly, for the outsized influence that Laban seems to exert in the early narrative of the Book of Mormon, this is the only direct statement uttered by him that Nephi records. With this false statement, foolish Laban breaks the Mosaic law to "not bear false witness against thy neighbour" (Exodus 20:16). Consequently, according to Mosaic law, whatever punishment the slanderer uttered against the slandered would turn back against him:

If a false witness rise up against any man to testify against him that which is wrong;

Then both the men, between whom the controversy is, shall stand before the Lord, before the priests and the judges, which shall be in those days;

And the judges shall make diligent inquisition: and, behold, if the witness be a false witness, and hath testified falsely against his brother;

Then shall ye do unto him, as he had thought to have done unto his brother: so shalt thou put the evil away from among you. (Deuteronomy 19:16–19)

Hence, the killing of Laban may have been lawfully justified.[44] In literary and legal irony, foolish Laban had spoken his own demise. And in this utterance, he had confirmed what the Wisdom tradition says about fools: they speak without thinking as "a false witness that speaketh lies, and he that soweth discord among brethren" (Proverbs 6:19), their mouths utter slander like "He that hideth hatred with lying lips, and he that uttereth a slander, is a fool. . . . Excellent speech becometh not a fool: much less do lying lips a prince" (Proverbs 10:18; 17:7).

The greatest obstacle to the wise is the fool. And the greatest obstacle for the preservation of wise sayings is the fool who does not understand the word of God or despises the word of God. Laban is the *nabal*, the fool who stands in the way of God's wisdom being transmitted through the ages. Hence, the wise man must kill the fool in order for wisdom to thrive.[45] And this is no ordinary death. The very head of the fool is removed so that his foolish thoughts can no longer sprout, his foolish words can no longer be uttered, and his foolish plans can no longer be devised. For Nephi and the Book of Mormon, this is but "the beginning of knowledge" (Proverbs 1:7).

And this is simply the beginning of the many ways that reading Nephi—indeed the entire Book of Mormon record—through the lens of Wisdom literature can lead to expansive and fruitful new insights and meaning.

## Conclusion

This chapter attempts to demonstrate that Nephi's writings appear to be deeply influenced by Israelite and ancient Middle Eastern Wisdom tradition themes. There are many Wisdom themes connecting the Book of Mormon to the Old Testament, though this chapter has focused on only five of those Wisdom themes that appear in 1 Nephi. Additional study will reveal many more connections between the Book of Mormon and the Wisdom literature tradition of ancient Israel.[46]

If the Wisdom tradition is a foundation for Nephi's scribal capabilities and outlook, perhaps the principles and literary skills represented by the scribal Wisdom tradition constitute the "learning of the Jews" that Nephi references so early in his record. Hence, if Nephi's record is a record of the learning of the Jews—a record of wisdom—we would be wise to read it with *Wisdom*.

# BECOMING A MAN OF GOD LIKE NEPHI[47]

By Taylor Halverson, PhD, and Ryan Brower

IN A WORLD THAT SENDS so many false and destructive messages to young men about what it really means to be a man, the scriptures are a powerful source of light and truth, providing stirring examples of what it means to be a man and the process for becoming a man.

Jesus's invitations to His disciples include these calls: "Therefore, what manner of men ought ye to be? Verily I say unto you, even as I am" (3 Nephi 27:27) and "Be ye therefore perfect, even as your Father which is in heaven is perfect" (Matthew 5:48). But what is that process of becoming the type of man that Jesus Christ is?

Again, we can turn to the scriptures for powerful examples.

One of the great scriptural heroes is the prophet Nephi, son of Lehi. He constitutes a great example of what it means to be a man. How did he grow from being a young man to becoming a man of God?

Nephi provides us with two bookends; between the two we can watch the process and learn the principles of making the transition from a young man to a man of God. Nephi identifies himself as being exceedingly young (see 1 Nephi 2:16); just two chapters later, Nephi describes himself as a man large in stature, having received much strength from the Lord (see 1 Nephi 4:31). What happened between those two scriptures that caused Nephi's significant transition from being a young man to being a man of God?

Let's explore the episodes that Nephi shared with us and learn the principles that we can apply to our lives so that we can become men—no longer young men, but men of God:

1. Pray to gain a personal testimony.
2. Share your testimony with others.
3. Be willing to do whatever the Lord commands you.
4. Have confidence that God will prepare a way for you to accomplish your mission.
5. Use the scriptures to build confidence and trust in God.
6. Follow the Spirit.

## 1. Pray to gain a personal testimony.

After Lehi fled Jerusalem with his family at the command of the Lord, he pitched his tent in a valley near a river. There, Lehi exhorted his two oldest sons, Laman and Lemuel, to keep the commandments:

> He spake unto Laman, saying: O that thou mightest be like unto this river, continually running into the fountain of all righteousness! And he also spake unto Lemuel: O that thou mightest be like unto this valley, firm and steadfast, and immovable in keeping the commandments of the Lord! (1 Nephi 2:9–10)

Nephi explained that his two oldest brothers were unwilling to listen to the voice of God through their prophet-father Lehi. What did Nephi do? Describing himself as being exceedingly young, he decided to put his questions and concerns to God in prayer. He sought his own testimony of the truth:

> And it came to pass that I, Nephi, being exceedingly young, nevertheless being large in stature, and also having great desires to know of the mysteries of God, wherefore, I did cry unto the Lord; and behold he did visit me, and did soften my heart that I did believe all the words which had been spoken by my father; wherefore, I did not rebel against him like unto my brothers. (1 Nephi 2:16)

The result? God answered Nephi's prayer and softened his heart so that Nephi believed the words of his father.

Young men who want to be men should, like Nephi, turn to God in prayer. God will answer your prayers and soften your heart, and in the process of receiving personal revelation from God, you will increase in honor and virtue and become more like God.

## 2. Share your testimony with others.

After Nephi received his own testimony, he shared it with others. His older brother Sam willingly listened and believed. But not everyone accepted Nephi's testimony, particularly Laman and Lemuel. Nephi prayed again to God earnestly, this time not to gain a testimony but on behalf of those whom he loved, desiring that they also would receive a testimony of the truth. In response to Nephi's desire for others to receive the truth, the Lord promised him marvelous blessings of a promised land and that Nephi would be a teacher to his brothers:

> Blessed art thou, Nephi, because of thy faith, for thou hast sought me diligently, with lowliness of heart.
>
> And inasmuch as ye shall keep my commandments, ye shall prosper, and shall be led to a land of promise; yea, even a land which I have prepared for you; yea, a land which is choice above all other lands.
>
> And inasmuch as thy brethren shall rebel against thee, they shall be cut off from the presence of the Lord.
>
> And inasmuch as thou shalt keep my commandments, thou shalt be made a ruler and a teacher over thy brethren.
>
> For behold, in that day that they shall rebel against me, I will curse them even with a sore curse, and they shall have no power over thy seed except they shall rebel against me also.
>
> And if it so be that they rebel against me, they shall be a scourge unto thy seed, to stir them up in the ways of remembrance. (1 Nephi 2:19–24)

## 3. Be willing to do whatever the Lord commands you.

After these experiences, Lehi commanded Nephi and his brothers to return to Jerusalem to seek the plates of brass from Laban. In contrast to Laman and Lemuel, who murmured and complained, Nephi immediately responded with faithful obedience:

I will go and do the things which the Lord hath commanded, for I know that the Lord giveth no commandments unto the children of men, save he shall prepare a way for them that they may accomplish the thing which he commandeth them. (1 Nephi 3:7)

## 4. Have confidence that God will prepare a way for you to accomplish your mission.

As we know, Laban was entirely unwilling to give the plates of brass to Nephi and his brothers. After Laban rejected Laman, some of Nephi's brothers wanted to return to Lehi in the wilderness. Nephi instead encouraged them with faith and testimony that God would help them fulfill the mission He had given them. In response, they went to their land of inheritance to gather together their precious things:

> But behold I said unto them that: As the Lord liveth, and as we live, we will not go down unto our father in the wilderness until we have accomplished the thing which the Lord hath commanded us.
>
> Wherefore, let us be faithful in keeping the commandments of the Lord; therefore let us go down to the land of our father's inheritance, for behold he left gold and silver, and all manner of riches. And all this he hath done because of the commandments of the Lord. (1 Nephi 3:15–16)

Unfortunately, Laban threatened their lives, and Nephi and his brothers had to flee, leaving their gold, silver, and precious things in Laban's possession.

## 5. Use the scriptures to build confidence and trust in God.

Laman and Lemuel made the situation worse by physically and verbally abusing Sam and Nephi. An angel of the Lord stopped the abuse, but Laman and Lemuel still murmured. Under these terrible circumstances, Nephi quoted scripture, reminding his brothers of the stories from the Old Testament in which God had miraculously saved His people from the mighty Egyptians:

> Therefore let us go up; let us be strong like unto Moses; for he truly spake unto the waters of the Red Sea and they divided hither and thither, and our fathers came through,

out of captivity, on dry ground, and the armies of Pharaoh did follow and were drowned in the waters of the Red Sea.

Now behold ye know that this is true; and ye also know that an angel hath spoken unto you; wherefore can ye doubt? Let us go up; the Lord is able to deliver us, even as our fathers, and to destroy Laban, even as the Egyptians. (1 Nephi 4:2–3)

If God could save all the Israelites from the Egyptians, couldn't he save these brothers from one man, even Laban?

## 6. Follow the Spirit.

Nephi convinced his brothers to let him try again to obtain the plates from Laban. Nephi went into the city not knowing how he would obtain the plates, knowing only that God had sent him on a mission and that with the Spirit he could accomplish all things. He wrote, "And I was led by the Spirit, not knowing beforehand the things which I should do" (1 Nephi 4:6).

As Nephi went by night toward the house of Laban, he discovered Laban drunk in the street. The Spirit urged Nephi to kill Laban. After many long struggles in his own mind and with the Spirit of God, Nephi took Laban's sword and cut off his head. Soon thereafter, Nephi came upon Zoram, a servant of Laban. He convinced Zoram to give him the plates of brass and to accompany him to his brothers. As soon as Zoram realized that Nephi was impersonating Laban, Zoram tried to flee. But Nephi caught hold of him and held him fast, promising that if Zoram covenanted to come with Nephi and his brothers, he would be a free man. Significantly, Nephi attributed his ability to hold Zoram and convince him with a covenant to not flee to the fact that he had now become a man, having received much strength of the Lord: "And now I, Nephi, being a man large in stature, and also having received much strength of the Lord . . ." (1 Nephi 4:31).

# IN COVER OF DARKNESS (1 NEPHI 4): EVIDENCES FOR THE BOOK OF MORMON[48]

THE BOOK OF MORMON PROVIDES many small or subtle clues that are relevant to its authenticity as an ancient record. The story of Nephi's confrontation with Laban contains some of these often unnoticed, yet relevantly essential details.

A reader of the Book of Mormon might ask, "How is it after the death of Laban, Nephi put on Laban's clothes, and Zoram didn't see what a mess the clothes were? Shouldn't that have tipped Zoram off that something was out of place, that there was a problem?"

That's a great question.

The small details in the Book of Mormon are significant and are easy to overlook. Particularly intriguing is that occasionally we hear Book of Mormon authors saying that they are careful not to include extraneous details in the record.

So, why the apparently extraneous details? Because upon closer inspection, we see that these details matter to the truthfulness of the story. The story of Nephi and Laban provides a rich example.

When Nephi encountered Laban, we learn that Laban was drunk (see 1 Nephi 4:7). If Zoram later saw Laban's clothes, perhaps Zoram would have mistaken any blood on the clothes for spilled wine. More likely is that the darkness of night meant Zoram couldn't see a thing. No amount of blood-stained clothing would be visible in the darkness of an ancient Jerusalem night. Modern-day people don't typically appreciate how truly dark nighttime is without any artificial light.

And how do we know that it was night? Nephi includes as a small detail, almost as an afterthought, this seemingly innocuous statement as he narrates his entry into the city:

*And it was by night*; and I caused that they should hide themselves without the walls. And after they had hid themselves, I, Nephi, crept into the city and went forth towards the house of Laban. (1 Nephi 4:5; emphasis added)

Nephi's confrontation with Laban is one of many stories in the Book of Mormon that contains subtle, yet essential clues to the authenticity of the Book of Mormon.

# WHAT WE KNOW ABOUT ONE OF THE MOST PROMINENT MOTHERS MENTIONED IN THE BOOK OF MORMON[49]

By Taylor Halverson, PhD, and Camille Fronk Olson, PhD

SARIAH IS ONE OF THE few named women in the Book of Mormon. Her contribution in the family dynamics of Lehi's party was crucial to the success of the journey to the promised land.

Based on clues from the Book of Mormon, Lehi had wealth and standing in the Jerusalem community. That would mean that Sariah would have likely had a comfortable dwelling, perhaps even some servants. In her responsibilities as the matriarch of the family, she likely managed all domestic operations, including resources to maintain the family home. She probably had a network of female friends who provided mutual support. She had much that anyone could desire for a stable, happy, prosperous life—a prosperous life she left mostly behind to enter a forbidding wilderness.

Even today, the Judean wilderness and the Arabian peninsula are not accommodating places for humans. Water and food are scarce. The heat can be unbearable. The possibility of highway robbery is real. Significant daily physical toil is essential to maintain life and to get from one place to another. Wind and sand are constant elements. All belongings must be carried by humans or pack animals, the latter of which have similar needs as humans have for water and food. In addition, centuries-old traditions of nomadic life in the ancient Middle East suggest that women performed the bulk of daily work in camp, including packing and setting up tents, caring for children and livestock, and cooking.

We may struggle to imagine the difficulties Sariah and her family suffered, especially considering that we have speedy travel with cars and airplanes. We have air conditioning and heat on demand. And we have so much water and food that more people in our society die from too much rather than the lack of it.

Yet even with such conveniences, modern-day family trips and outings are rarely free of grumbling and complaining. That makes it easy, then, to sympathize with Sariah's occasional complaining. The increased hardships she must have assumed to maintain wilderness living for eight years were daunting. Sariah's experience was challenging physically as well as spiritually.

After several weeks of travel into the wilderness, Sariah's four sons returned to Jerusalem in obedience to a revelation her husband received from God. Danger lurked everywhere around Jerusalem. Inhabitants wanted to kill Lehi (and perhaps other members of his family, including the returning sons), and Laban was a military leader, "a mighty man, and he can command fifty, yea, even he can slay fifty" (1 Nephi 3:31).

That posed its own risks; but there were more. Traveling in the desert itself posed many risks. The round-trip journey for Sariah's sons could have been as far as five hundred miles and would have required a minimum of three weeks.

That is a lot of time for Sariah to fret in the desert, to worry and wonder *What has become of my sons? Are they alive? Have they become food for wild beasts? Have the inhabitants of Jerusalem detained them? Executed them?* With no access to modern forms of communication, Sariah would have no status updates on her boys except through revelation.

During these difficult times, Sariah complained regularly to Lehi, saying, "Behold thou hast led us forth from the land of our inheritance, and my sons are no more, and we perish in the wilderness" (1 Nephi 5:2).

Lehi comforted Sariah with his trust in God, telling her, "I know that the Lord will deliver my sons out of the hands of Laban, and bring them down again unto us in the wilderness" (1 Nephi 5:5).

Though Sariah trusted Lehi's witness from God enough to leave everything behind in Jerusalem, her faith was now tested beyond what her husband's faith could compensate with the threat of losing all four of her sons. She needed to learn for herself to trust God that He "will show unto you that the tender mercies of the Lord are over all those whom he hath chosen, because of their faith, to make them mighty even unto the power of deliverance" (1 Nephi 1:20).

Sariah needed her own testimony that God would fulfill His promises. This was her moment of testing.

When her sons returned from the long errand, Sariah "was exceedingly glad, for she truly had mourned" because she thought her sons had perished (1 Nephi 5:1).

Nephi recorded a direct quote from his mother, Sariah, that reflects her newfound spiritual independence: "Now I know of a surety. . . ." (1 Nephi 5:8). In this quote, her expression of faith plays upon the meaning of her own name in a chiastic structure, as we saw displayed in the chapter on Book of Mormon names.

Nephi's record indicates the importance of his mother, not just his father, having unshakeable faith if the family was to succeed in their mission. Both were needed to shape a family that would be instrumental in producing a record that would invite generations of God's children to come to Christ.

Sariah's humanity is appealing. Her testimony is invigorating. Her faithfulness to God in the face of the difficult realities of life, even though she had moments of complaining, can encourage all of us each day, as President Gordon B. Hinckley challenged us, "to try a little harder to be a little better" ("We Have a Work to Do," *Ensign*, May 1995).

# FINDING THE FIRST USE OF THE NAME CHRIST IN THE BOOK OF MORMON[50]

SOME YEARS AGO, WHILE TEACHING a Book of Mormon class at Brigham Young University, I discussed with the class titles and names for Jesus Christ used throughout the Book of Mormon. As is well known, the Book of Mormon is saturated with references to Jesus Christ.

We reviewed some of the names for Christ used early in Nephi's record: Messiah, Holy One of Israel, Lord, God, Lord God Almighty, God of Israel, God of Abraham, God of Isaac, God of Jacob, Savior, Redeemer, and Son of God. It is clear that many of these titles originated in an Old Testament religious context.

We also discussed the frequency of the use of the name *Christ*, which appears nearly four hundred times throughout the Book of Mormon.

As we studied this topic further, I had the following exchange with the students, trying to invite them to read the Book of Mormon more carefully by looking for details, asking questions, and seeking answers:

> **Dr. Halverson**: "Where is the first use of the name Christ in the Book of Mormon?"
>
> **Students**: After some searching, and especially with the help of electronic devices, the students responded that the first use was in 2 Nephi 10:3.
>
> **Dr. Halverson**: "Great find. Now, if Christ is the central figure of the Book of Mormon, why isn't the name Christ used until seventy-eight pages into the Book of Mormon? We are nearly 15 percent through the Book of Mormon, and this is the first time that the name Christ is used. Why is that?"

**Students**: After doing some careful reading, they responded: "Because Jacob explains in 2 Nephi 10:3 'for in the last night the angel spake unto me that this should be his name.'"

**Dr. Halverson**: "Excellent. But this raises other questions. Why didn't Jacob know Christ's name before that time? For example, why didn't Lehi or Nephi teach Jacob Christ's name or title? Why did it take an angel to reveal this to Jacob? Shouldn't Lehi and Nephi have received that revelation as the prophet-leaders? Shouldn't they have already known the name of Christ?"

**Students**: The students were stumped by the questions.

**Dr. Halverson**: "I'll provide some context that may help answer these questions. The word *Christ* is Greek. The same term in Hebrew is *Messiah*, which Nephi uses on a number of occasions."

**Students**: Beginning to comprehend: "Oh, Nephi and Jacob didn't know Greek. They would not have used a Greek word to talk about Him when they came from a Hebrew-speaking culture. They would have used other names for Him from their own language and culture."

**Dr. Halverson**: "Exactly. That is why other phrases, familiar in the Old Testament world, were so often used by Nephi. Nephi didn't know Christ's name in Greek. So Nephi used a title from his Hebrew background that referred to Jesus Christ—*Messiah*. It wasn't until Nephi's younger brother Jacob received revelation about the name *Christ* that suddenly Old-Testament-world phrases like *Messiah* fall out of use in the Book of Mormon and *Christ* becomes one of the primary terms used to name Him. In fact, the Hebrew term *Messiah* is used twenty-eight times by Nephi (not including his quotes of Isaiah) before Jacob's revelation about the name *Christ*. But after that Nephi only uses the term *Messiah* ten more times. And it is striking to note that Jacob never uses the term *Messiah*. After the death of Nephi, *Messiah* is used only three times in the remainder of the Book of Mormon. Before Jacob's revelation, *Christ* is never used in the Book of Mormon. After Jacob's revelation, *Christ* is used nearly four hundred times, with the highest percentage going to the writers Jacob, Mormon, and Moroni."

My conversation with the students was an enlightening one. I've since learned more.

Our discussion is based on our current versions of the Book of Mormon but does not take into consideration the original manuscript of the Book of Mormon. Professor Royal Skousen of Brigham Young University has spent his career studying the many small differences between the original manuscript Joseph Smith dictated to Oliver Cowdery, the printer's manuscript created by Cowdery, and the official version of the Book of Mormon we have today. Those small differences go from the mundane to the intriguing. (To learn more, look for the volumes in Dr. Skousen's series *The Book of Mormon: The Earliest Text*.) My point here is to not distract us with these interesting questions but to simply highlight that sometimes our discoveries about the Book of Mormon may need to be tempered or updated with new information.

For example, as I said above, my conversation with the students did not take into consideration what the original manuscript of the Book of Mormon said. We were only reading what was in the 1981 edition of the Book of Mormon. If we review the original manuscript and the original version of the Book of Mormon from 1830, we learn that the first time the name *Jesus Christ* is used is in 1 Nephi 12:18 during Nephi's revelatory experience with an angel who showed him the tree of life and many other things. In the 1837 edition of the Book of Mormon, Joseph Smith changed *Jesus Christ* to *Messiah* in 1 Nephi 12:18. Joseph Smith never explained why he made the change, but that change updates my conclusions with the students.

Instead of concluding that Nephi never spoke the name of Christ because he didn't know until his brother Jacob revealed it, we'll have to make other conclusions. Perhaps Nephi felt more familiar with the Hebrew term *Messiah* (with which he had grown up) rather than using the foreign (though revealed) term *Christ*. Perhaps after a "second witness" revealed the name *Christ* (Nephi was one witness and his brother Jacob was now a second witness), Nephi felt more comfortable to begin using that term.

Whatever the case may be, a strong argument can be made that Nephi originally preferred to use the Hebrew word with which he had grown up, *Messiah*, to speak about Christ instead of using the foreign Greek word *Christ*. And after both he and his brother received revelation that the Messiah would be called *Christ*, Nephi began to use the word *Christ* more often while minimizing his use of the word *Messiah*. As someone who had grown up in an Old Testament, Hebrew-speaking culture, that seems like a reasonable expectation to have of Nephi. Of course, with more thought, time, effort, and additional insights and evidence, we may discover even better explanations.

Nephi is an entirely real character given his time, place, and upbringing. It is highly unlikely that Joseph Smith, a farm boy from upstate New York, could have invented an ancient character like Nephi and then so capably aligned Nephi with the ancient culture from which he came (especially since Joseph Smith would have known little about such a culture). This is further evidence that the Book of Mormon should be taken seriously as an authentic witness that Jesus is the Christ, the One who can save us from our sins.

# NEPHI'S GRAND VISION: 1 NEPHI 11–14[51]

## Introduction

NEPHI PROVIDES ONE OF THE most remarkable visionary experiences recorded in scripture. In the short sweep of four chapters, he unveils patterns of the
plan of salvation woven into the threads of world history. In the process he
also elucidates four vital gospel themes that appear throughout scripture and
in the words of modern-day prophets. A careful study of Nephi's grand vision in 1 Nephi 11–14 will prepare us to understand the patterns of the plan
of salvation and the gospel as they are manifested in history and throughout
the scriptures.

Let's look at the vision from three perspectives. The first two perspectives are "apocalyptic literature" and "salvation history." The last perspective
involves four key themes present in Nephi's vision, which are also found
repeatedly throughout the Book of Mormon. When we understand these
four key themes, we have made significant inroads to understanding patterns
and themes throughout the Book of Mormon, other scripture, and history.
In preparation for carefully investigating Nephi's vision, let us study each of
the three perspectives.

## Perspective 1—Apocalyptic Literature

One way to enhance our understanding of 1 Nephi 11–14 is to read it
from a literary perspective—that is, to see the literary features and structure
around which these passages are built. Literary features guide us in interpreting a text. No one who reads the phrase "Once upon a time" would think
they were reading a business report or a thank-you card.

Literary features come in many forms. Some are epistolary, such as the
Pauline letters, which have formulaic greetings and salutations marking the

introduction and conclusion of the epistle. Other literary features are hortatory (for example, exhortation, counsel, commandment) in style, often couched in command forms such as the famous President Spencer W. Kimball dictum, "Do it!" The book of James in the New Testament is a lucid example of hortatory style; more than half the book is written in command form.

Most of us are familiar with the literary style of chiasmus that generously adorns the structure of the Book of Mormon text. Another literary style that is relatively unknown is that of "apocalyptic." We are familiar with the book of Daniel and the book of Revelation. Both these books are written in the literary genre of apocalyptic. So too is 1 Nephi 11–14. Recognizing the apocalyptic literary genre is one way to help us generate meaning from this Book of Mormon text.[52] The most salient features of apocalyptic literature are:

- A prophetic figure (such as Daniel, John, or Nephi)
- Visions or revelation
  —disclosed by an angel or heavenly being
  —occurs on a high mountain or on a heavenly journey
- Divine interpretations
  —of history
     often in a chronological, salvation history format, where the events of history are interpreted as leading up to the triumph of God over evil when a new era of peace is inaugurated
  —of symbols
     sometimes bizarre and strange, such as in the book of Revelation animal imagery
        Lamb = Christ
        Dragon/snake = Satan
- Prophecy or predictions of the future
  —beginning with the time of the prophet and progressing into the future until the end of one era and the inauguration of a new era
  —particular focus on end times, or the times in history when an era of oppression ends and a new era of peace prevails

As you read this outline, you probably recognized that the literary style of 1 Nephi 11–14 shares these apocalyptic features. To be able to see the scriptures from multiple perspectives enlarges our understanding.

**Perspective 2—Salvation History**

There are many ways to understand history. If this was not the case, history departments at universities across the world would quickly close. Among the many ways available for understanding history,[53] one approach is highly appropriate for our study of the Book of Mormon, an approach much neglected by the rest of the world. It is the approach of "salvation history," or reading history from the perspective that there is a plan of salvation for the inhabitants of this world and that events can best be understood and interpreted within that perspective.

This "salvation history" or "plan of salvation" perspective is particularly helpful for understanding the Book of Mormon, both on a macro and micro level. When we are buried in the stories and details of Book of Mormon events, we can always step back and place things in their broader "plan of salvation" perspective. This approach will help us navigate one of the most remarkable revelations ever recorded: 1 Nephi 11–14.

Incidentally, the four key themes detailed below are components of the "salvation history" perspective.

**Perspective 3—Themes in Nephi's Vision and the Book of Mormon**

One of the reasons why Nephi's vision is so valuable to read and understand is because it traces four major groups of doctrinal themes that are successively repeated throughout the pages of the Book of Mormon and in the words of modern-day prophets.[54]

*Theme 1* includes the birth, ministry, and Atonement of Jesus Christ, which is the focus of 1 Nephi 11.

*Theme 2* features the divisions, pride, and strife among the families of the earth that occur because of humanity's fallen condition, successive apostasies, and the persecution of the righteous. 1 Nephi 12 focuses mainly on this theme.

*Theme 3* speaks of divine messengers (such as Christ or an angel) visiting the inhabitants of the earth to share the gospel message. This gospel preaching leads to the preparation for and fulfillment of successive restorations of the gospel. These restorations culminate in the final and last restoration of the fullness of times, which is occurring in our day. This theme prevails in 1 Nephi 13.

*Theme 4* describes the cataclysmic events at the turning of an era, God's victory over the forces of evil, the salvation of the righteous, and the ushering in of a new age of peace and righteousness. Patterns of this theme dominate 1 Nephi 14.

I will tie together the three perspectives described above, including the four major gospel themes, to inform our overall understanding of 1 Nephi 11–14. My approach will be to show these ideas playing out in the text, while offering commentary on various verses of Nephi's vision.

I pause on one final note before we delve into Nephi's vision. I wish to review the powerful yet simple approach Nephi employed to receive this stunning revelation. In Nephi's own words, he explains:

> For it came to pass after I had desired to know the things
> that my father had seen [in a vision], and believing that the Lord
> was able to make them known unto me, as I sat pondering in
> mine heart I was caught away in the Spirit of the Lord, yea, into
> an exceedingly high mountain, which I never had before seen,
> and upon which I never had before set my foot. (1 Nephi 11:1)

This verse presents us with key principles for receiving revelation:
- **I desired** to know
- **I believed** that the Lord was able to make them known unto me
- **I pondered**

As we study the scriptures, let us faithfully follow Nephi's example.

## Wickedness and Apostasy—1 Nephi 12

*1 Nephi 12:1–3*

In these verses, Nephi sees much of the history of his descendants and the descendants of his brothers Laman and Lemuel between his day and the coming of Christ. Unfortunately, that history was marked with contention, strife, and wickedness. These verses are representative of the second theme listed above (pride, strife, and apostasy).

*1 Nephi 12:4–5*

These two verses are marked with the cataclysmic events indicative of a change from one era to the next when the wicked are wiped away and the righteous are granted a time of peace. In these verses specifically, Nephi sees the destruction that would take place in the promised land among his people at the death of Jesus Christ (see 3 Nephi 8). These patterns are representative of the fourth theme (God's triumph over evil).

*1 Nephi 12:6–12*

Nephi sees terrible destructions and calamities, all of which are preparatory for the advent of Christ on the earth among His own people. The gospel
message is once again spread abroad through disciples chosen by Christ (see
3 Nephi 11, 19). An age of wickedness and apostasy passes away, marked
by a restoration and a new age of peace and righteousness, indicative of the
third and fourth themes (restoration and peace; see also 4 Nephi).

We learn in these verses that at the final judgment, the twelve disciples chosen
by Christ on the American continent will be judges over the people of Nephi.
Furthermore, these disciples have been purged of all staining sin through faith,
repentance, and the power of the Atonement. In this chapter, the use of the word
Lamb (a sacrificial symbol of purity, innocence, and meekness) refers to Jesus
Christ, just as it does in the apocalyptic book of Revelation.

*1 Nephi 12:13–23*

The final verses of 1 Nephi 12 are representative again of the second
theme (pride, disunity, apostasy, and wickedness). It is a common pattern in
history that after a people have been long blessed with prosperity, peace, and
righteousness, they eventually turn to pride and wickedness. After hundreds
of years of righteous peace inaugurated by the visit of Christ, Nephi saw that
future generations of his descendants would fall into this wickedness and
apostasy (see Mormon 1–6). The angel explains this portion of history as a
time of darkness and abomination.

We also receive in these verses divine interpretation concerning Lehi's
dream and how this describes the history of Lehi's descendants (see verses
16–18). The mists of darkness are the temptations of the devil, the river is
representative of hell, and the large and spacious building is representative of
pride, the same type of pride that brought the mighty Nephite nation down
low into the dust of death.

## Restoration Preparation—1 Nephi 13

*1 Nephi 13:1–11*

The opening eleven verses of chapter 13 continue the same ideas of the
second theme. The angelic informant shows Nephi the history of the world
after the time of Christ. Many nations and kingdoms arise, often warring
against each other and most walking in the ways of apostasy. Representative
of this apostasy was the formation of a great and abominable church that

promoted pride, promiscuity, and wickedness, symbolized in this vision by silks, scarlet, gold, and harlots (see verses 6–9). Moving forward to 1 Nephi 14:10, the angel explains more clearly how to identify this church (lest we seek to label any one denomination as "the Great and Abominable Church"):

> Behold there are save two churches only; the one is the church of the Lamb of God, and the other is the church of the devil; wherefore, whoso belongeth not to the church of the Lamb of God belongeth to that great church, which is the mother of abominations; and she is the whore of all the earth. (1 Nephi 14:10)

This abominable church warred against and persecuted the Saints and, as Nephi learned later in chapter 13, corrupted the precious word of God.

### 1 Nephi 13:12–19

At this point in his vision, Nephi has seen more than two thousand years of world history (roughly from 600 BC to AD 1500). The angel now focuses Nephi's attention on one man among the Gentiles[55] who was wrought upon by the Holy Spirit to cross the waters from the Old World to the New World: Christopher Columbus. How fitting that his name is Christopher, for the Latin root of that name means "bearer of Christ."

The history of salvation as seen in Nephi's vision now highlights the role that Gentiles would and do play in the restoration of the gospel and the gathering in of the scattered tribes of Israel to Zion. These verses highlight the discovering and colonization of the Americas, the Revolutionary War, and the establishment of the United States of America.

### 1 Nephi 13:20–29

In these verses, the angel explains to Nephi the history and transmission of the biblical record. It is called a book that proceeds forth from the mouth of a Jew (see verse 24), not literally meaning that one Jew wrote the entire Bible, but rather those who composed the biblical texts are to be identified as members of the house of Israel and Judah. The angel explains that the Bible had originally been full of pure doctrine and truth, but that over the years as it was transmitted, corruptions were introduced to the point that many of the plain and precious truths were smudged with misunderstanding or were deleted altogether. Because of these textual imperfections, many of the Gentiles had erroneous beliefs, ideas, and lifestyles, leaving them under the influence of the adversary. Verses 26–30 are examples of the pattern of apostasy found in the second theme (pride, strife, and apostasy).

### *1 Nephi 13:30–42*

These final verses of the chapter again focus on the third theme (divine messengers and restoration). Nephi sees that even though God had raised up the Gentiles to prepare the way for the restoration of all things, He did not grant them power to completely destroy other covenant people (such as the descendants of the Lamanites who still lived throughout the Americas). In explaining the history of salvation, the angel declares to Nephi that God will do His work to save the ancient covenant people—as well as the stumbling and blind Gentiles—who were blinded because of biblical imperfections. God's promise was to bring forth the precious parts of the gospel after the Gentiles had persecuted and hunted the ancient covenant people.

As the vision continues, Nephi sees that many books of scripture proclaiming the pure doctrine of Christ come forward in the latter days as companions to the book that proceeded forth from the mouth of a Jew (the Bible). By means of these records, truth will be established, error dissolved, and doctrines clarified. Nephi learns that the central message of these scriptures is "that the Lamb of God is the Son of the Eternal Father, and the Savior of the world; and that all men must come unto him, or they cannot be saved" (1 Nephi 13:40). A promise yet to be fulfilled is that Christ will manifest Himself to all people in the latter days, both Jew and Gentile alike.

## Righteous Triumphant—1 Nephi 14

The three chapters of this vision progressively focus on apostasy, restoration, and the eventual establishment of God's kingdom of righteousness on the earth. Chapter 14 speaks almost exclusively in terms of the fourth theme: God's victory over the forces of evil, salvation of the righteous, and the ushering in of a new age of peace and righteousness.

### *1 Nephi 14:1–2*

The theme of restoration and gospel preaching to the Gentiles continues through verse two of this chapter. God promises Nephi that at some point in history the Gentiles will have their stumbling block removed (including their false ideas, prejudices, and erroneous lifestyles). When the truth is offered to them and when they gladly receive it, they will be numbered among the house of Israel. They will no longer be called strangers and foreigners, but children of the King. This is our day, the day of the Gentiles, when the fullness of the truth is being promulgated. We have the opportunity to put aside our fears and false beliefs in order to accept with full humility the saving truths of pure love.

### 1 Nephi 14:3–10

Beginning in verse three, we see the mighty acts of God at work to destroy the forces and structures of evil in preparation for His kingdom to spread across the earth; the wicked will be ensnared by their own devices. Nevertheless, those who choose darkness over light, who refuse to heed the warning voice and see the light of accumulating revelation of truth, will be grouped with the great and abominable church, whose founder is the devil himself and whose members are comprised of all those who refused the loving charity of their God and Father.

### 1 Nephi 14:11–17

As the vision of the last days passes before Nephi's view, he witnesses that both the Church of God and the abominable church spread throughout the earth, but because of the craft of the devil, the Saints of God are in the minority. Wrath and war from God will be poured out upon the wicked, the righteous will be armed with the strength of God, and it is at this moment that the promises and covenants of the ages will be fulfilled. Nephi witnesses that God will do His marvelous work among the children of men. This is our day.

### 1 Nephi 14:18–30

Nephi concludes his revelatory vision with a description of the Apostle John, who was commissioned by the Lord to write many things concerning the last days and the end of the world. Nephi too saw these things but was forbidden to record them. Instead, he ends his account standing as a second witness to the things his father saw in a dream and reaffirming the veracity of his own recorded visionary experience.

## Conclusion

In a nutshell, the apocalyptic vision of Nephi presented in 1 Nephi 11–14 contains the principal parts of the restored gospel. In chapter 11, the atoning mission of Jesus Christ is set forth. Chapter 12 details the historically repeated cycle of apostasy and wickedness. In chapter 13, we see one grand example of how the Lord prepares the earth to receive the truth, focusing specifically on the events that lead to the Restoration in the last days and the dispensation of the fullness of times. And chapter 14 concludes with the desire of the ages: the Lord's Second Coming, the ushering in of millennial peace when wickedness and oppression are terminated and the righteous are saved into the everlasting rest of the Lord. These are some of the most important themes and doctrines of the gospel. We find them throughout the Book of Mormon, other scriptures, and in the testimonies of modern-day prophets. That we can access these truths by means of this marvelous yet compact vision is a wonder.

# RESURRECTING DEEP SLEEPERS: 2 NEPHI 1[56]

HAVE YOU EVER WONDERED IF you would sleep through the sound of the trumpets on resurrection morning (see D&C 45:45–46)? Or have you ever considered that sleeping patterns of today may adversely affect you tomorrow? From a spiritual perspective, these are essential questions about our personal salvation. Fortunately, the scriptures provide us powerful insights about the symbolic meanings of resurrection that teach us how to overcome and avoid an "endless sleep" (Mormon 9:13) that could befall us at any time.

Quite early, the Book of Mormon exposes us to the idea of spiritual resurrection. Upon arrival in the promised land and in preparation for his own death, Lehi gave counsel and blessings to each of his children. Laman and Lemuel had experienced considerable difficulty keeping the commandments, which left them vulnerable to the full measure of God's justice. As their father, Lehi feared for their eternal welfare, so accordingly he exhorted them to repent using bold commands and figurative language:

> O that ye would awake; awake from a deep sleep, yea,
> even from the sleep of hell, and shake off the awful chains
> by which ye are bound, which are the chains which bind the
> children of men, that they are carried away captive down to
> the eternal gulf of misery and woe. (2 Nephi 1:13)

For Lehi, it appeared that his sons had already fallen asleep spiritually and needed a good rousing. Lehi expressed "all the feeling of a tender parent" who desired that his children "would hearken to his words, that perhaps the Lord would be merciful to them, and not cast them off" (1 Nephi 8:37). Because death was an approaching reality for him, Lehi understood the final totality of death "from whence no traveler can return" (2 Nephi 1:14) and knew that spiritual death was just as binding. So he continued to exhort his sons, saying:

> Awake! and arise from the dust, and hear the words of a trembling parent . . . arise from the dust . . . that ye may not come down into captivity . . .
> Awake, my sons; put on the armor of righteousness. Shake off the chains with which ye are bound, and come forth out of obscurity, and arise from the dust. (2 Nephi 1:14, 21, 23)

In essence, Lehi commanded his sons to spiritually resurrect. He made his message doubly clear by repeating themes of life, such as "awake" and "arise," juxtaposed to themes of death, such as "deep sleep" and "dust." There is great power in Lehi's approach. This pattern of speaking and awakening occurs in ancient literature, such as the Creation accounts where God speaks and Creation responds.[57]

Years later this theme was picked up and developed further by Jacob, most likely based on his father's teachings. Referring to the wickedness of the people of his own day, Jacob cried:

> O my brethren, hearken unto my words; arouse the faculties of your souls; shake yourselves that ye may awake from the slumber of death; and loose yourselves from the pains of hell that ye may not become angels to the devil, to be cast into that lake of fire and brimstone which is the second death. (Jacob 3:11)

Clearly, Jacob and Lehi understood that "deep sleep" was the sleep of death and that one must always be spiritually watchful and vigilant (see 1 Thessalonians 5:6) so as not to succumb to the enticings and flatteries of the devil. To do so would bring about the "pains of hell." That Nephi understood this principle of spiritual resurrection as well is evident through his own writings, which record his desire to not fall into spiritual sleep: "Awake, my soul! No longer droop in sin" (2 Nephi 4:28).

It is significant that the use of the phrase "deep sleep" in the Book of Mormon may derive from the Hebrew word *tardemah*.[58] *Tardemah* is employed in a variety of ways throughout the Old Testament. For example,

Proverbs 19:15 expresses *tardemah* as a consequence of spiritual slothfulness. The master poet Isaiah uses *tardemah* figuratively in Isaiah 29:10 to identify those who are insensitive to the Spirit, or past feeling. The Hebrew root word for *tardemah* is *radam*, which Psalms 76:6 expresses as that sleep called death.[59] The polar opposite of "deep sleep" is to be "awake." In their exhortations to the spiritually sleepy, Lehi and Jacob may have used the Hebrew root word *'ur*, which means to "rouse oneself to activity."[60]

Yet how is it that those with a full understanding of the gospel plan could fall into a spiritual coma? The nuances of the words *tardemah* and *radam* may suggest an answer. Those who have fallen into a deep spiritual sleep do so because they were insensitive and past feeling to the Spirit of God. This state is a result of slothfulness, having their ears closed to the things of God, which prevented them from putting on the armor of righteousness and shaking off the chains with which they were bound.[61]

There is only one way to arouse those who sleep in spiritual death: It's to do as Lehi did and call the sleepers in a loud voice of admonition and warning to "awake." Ultimately the responsibility lies with the deep sleeper to be the agent who actively responds to the call of spiritual resurrection. This is powerfully exemplified in the conversion story of Alma the Younger, who was stopped in his destructive path by the voice of God's angel (see Mosiah 27). Perhaps the voice was that of God Himself, since God is sometimes equated in the Old Testament with the phrase "the angel of the Lord." Alma fell and became as if he were dead; truly, he spiritually was. During those two days his soul died and then resurrected as he responded to God's call to "awake." In a later account, Alma tells us that he experienced the "pains of hell" until he remembered what his father had taught concerning Jesus Christ, who would come "to atone for the sins of the world" (Alma 36:17). Alma recorded:

> Now, as my mind caught hold upon this thought, I cried within my heart:
> O Jesus, thou Son of God, have mercy on me, who am in the gall of bitterness,
> and am encircled about by the everlasting chains of death.
> And now, behold, when I thought this, I could remember my pains no more . . . and oh, what joy, and what marvelous light I did behold. (Alma 36:18–20)

Alma had learned for himself through his own experience that spiritual death was real, but so was spiritual resurrection. He learned, as we must, that "now it is high time to awake out of sleep: for now is our salvation nearer than we believed. The night is far spent, the day is at hand: let us therefore cast off the works of darkness, and let us put on the armour of light" (Romans 13:11–12).

# JACOB'S MASTERFUL DISCOURSE:
## 2 NEPHI 6–10[62]

ONE OF THE MOST BEAUTIFUL and doctrinally significant discourses in the Book of Mormon was given in 2 Nephi 6–10 by Jacob, the brother of Nephi. The farewell speech of King Benjamin or the sermons of Jesus Christ when He visited the American continent are all well known. But seldom do we recognize that 2 Nephi 6–10 comprises a single lengthy gospel discourse.

The structure of Jacob's mighty speech is quite simple. 2 Nephi 6 serves as an introduction to his discourse, outlining the key themes that he wishes to talk about and establishing a framework for understanding and interpreting Isaiah 50–52:2. Jacob quotes these two Isaiah chapters in 2 Nephi 7 and 8. Next, Jacob moves to the main body of his discourse, found in chapter 9, to explain gospel principles and clarify the meaning of the words of Isaiah. He concludes his discourse in 2 Nephi 10, encouraging his listeners to live in joy and happiness because of the covenants and Atonement of the Lord.

The key themes and ideas of this powerful discourse are:

- the scattering and gathering of Israel
- the Messiah coming in the fullness of times to fulfill God's covenants of redemption
- the Messiah coming to teach the doctrines of salvation
- establishing the doctrines of salvation
- the second gathering of Israel preparatory for Christ's Second Coming on the earth
- knowing and living the gospel as a foundation for joy in this life

## 2 Nephi 6—Introduction to Jacob's Discourse

This chapter is an essential foundation for understanding the ensuing four chapters. Jacob lays out the purpose for his preaching and explains why he appeals to the words of Isaiah as he teaches his people. Verse 4 tells us that Jacob desires to speak of things as they are and things that are to come. In other words, he speaks of how the lives of his people fit into the overall picture of the plan of salvation and redemption of Israel (see verse 5). Then he turns to prophecies that are yet to be fulfilled, which will be a blessing to the posterity of his audience and to future generations of the earth's inhabitants (see verses 9–15).

Jacob explains that he will use Isaiah to speak of the present and the future with the explicit purpose that his people might learn and glorify the name of God. Specifically, Jacob reminds his people that they are of the house of Israel. Isaiah prophesied concerning the house of Israel, so his words are especially pertinent to the Nephites. The same holds true for us today. So just as Jacob likened all scriptures unto his people (following the example of Nephi), we too can liken these scriptures to our own lives.

What are the key themes and ideas that Jacob begins to clarify by using Isaiah? He focuses on the gathering and redemption of Israel and the Atonement wrought by the Holy One of Israel (Jesus Christ). God had dispersed covenant Israel due to their wickedness, yet He left a promise on their posterity that He would again gather them in and save them (see verses 6–7). The first gathering, Jacob explains, will occur during the ministry of Jesus Christ. But the people of Israel again rejected God and were once again scattered and afflicted (see verses 10–11). Jacob assures the people that despite suffering and affliction, those who repent and wait upon the Lord will be gathered in again a second time (see verses 13–14). This second gathering will be aided by the Gentiles, who will act as nursing kings and queens to Israel (see verses 6–7). We are in the midst of the second gathering today.

## 2 Nephi 7—God Will Fulfill His Covenants

Jacob appropriately quotes Isaiah 50 at this moment in his discourse. In this chapter, God reveals He will not forget Israel and He will not forget His covenants. Israel can trust in Him; He will save them. "O house of Israel, is my hand shortened at all that it cannot redeem, or have I no power to deliver?" (2 Nephi 7:2). The rest of the chapter describes God's mighty saving power and illustrates the loving compassion displayed by Isaiah as he submits to suffering in order to share the message of salvation for the covenant people:

> The Lord God hath opened mine ear, and I was not re-
> bellious, neither turned away back.
>
> I gave my back to the smiter, and my cheeks to them
> that plucked off the hair. I hid not my face from shame and
> spitting.
>
> For the Lord God will help. . . (2 Nephi 7:5–6, 9)

Isaiah's faith in God's saving capacity, even in the face of such suffering, certainly can provide reassurances to those of the house of Israel who may feel forsaken or that God had forgotten His covenant to gather them in. God's redeeming covenants are sure.

## 2 Nephi 8—Spiritual Courage to Covenant Israel

Jacob continues to quote from Isaiah in this chapter (compare to Isaiah 51–52:1-2), encouraging his own people to remember their heritage, to remember who they are in the sight of the Lord, to remember the covenants, to practice lives of righteousness, and to look forward with steadfast faith to the redemption God had promised. Following are some of the key ideas of this chapter:

*God's strength is mighty to save*

"Art thou not he who hath dried the sea, the waters of the great deep; that hath made the depths of the sea a way for the ransomed to pass over?" (2 Nephi 8:10). This clearly evokes the motif of Israel's deliverance from Egyptian bondage.

*God will gather His people*

"Therefore, the redeemed of the Lord shall return, and come with singing unto Zion; and everlasting joy and holiness shall be upon their heads; and they shall obtain gladness and joy; sorrow and mourning shall flee away" (2 Nephi 8:11).

*Israel should find comfort in the power of God*

"I am he; yea, I am he that comforteth you. Behold, who art thou, that thou shouldst be afraid of man, who shall die, and of the son of man, who shall be made like unto grass?" (2 Nephi 8:12).

*Israel should put aside their spiritual forgetfulness*

"And forgettest the Lord thy maker, that hath stretched forth the heavens, and laid the foundations of the earth, and hast feared continually every day, because of the fury of the oppressor, as if he were ready to destroy? And where is the fury of the oppressor?" (2 Nephi 8:13).

God rouses Israel to spiritual strength and wakefulness; Jerusalem will be restored and once again be called the city holy

"Awake, awake, put on thy strength, O Zion; put on thy beautiful garments, O Jerusalem, the holy city; for henceforth there shall no more come into thee the uncircumcised and the unclean" (2 Nephi 8:24).

## 2 Nephi 9—The Plan of Salvation

Transitioning from reading the words of Isaiah to interpreting them, Jacob explains, "And now, my beloved brethren, I have read these things that ye might know concerning the covenants of the Lord that he has covenanted with all the house of Israel" (2 Nephi 9:1). Not only has Isaiah spoken of these things, but all the holy prophets from the beginning of time have preached the gospel plan of salvation (see verse 2), which is to bring us joy and blessings (see verse 3).

What exactly is the plan of salvation? One of the finest doctrinal expositions on the plan of salvation ever recorded is found in 2 Nephi 9, and verses 5–8 offer a convincing summary:

> Yea, I know that ye know that in the body he shall show himself unto those at Jerusalem, from whence we came; for it is expedient that it should be among them; for it behooveth the great Creator that he suffereth himself to become subject unto man in the flesh, and die for all men, that all men might become subject unto him.
>
> For as death hath passed upon all men, to fulfil the merciful plan of the great Creator, there must needs be a power of resurrection, and the resurrection must needs come unto man by reason of the fall; and the fall came by reason of transgression; and because man became fallen they were cut off from the presence of the Lord.
>
> Wherefore, it must needs be an infinite atonement— save it should be an infinite atonement this corruption could

not put on incorruption. Wherefore, the first judgment which came upon man must needs have remained to an endless duration. And if so, this flesh must have laid down to rot and to crumble to its mother earth, to rise no more.

O the wisdom of God, his mercy and grace! For behold, if the flesh should rise no more our spirits must become subject to that angel who fell from before the presence of the Eternal God, and became the devil, to rise no more. (2 Nephi 9:5–8)

Jacob emphasizes the goodness and greatness of God for sending His Son, Jesus Christ, that we might overcome the twin monsters of death and hell. Due to the fall of mankind in the Garden of Eden, we are on this earth with corruptible, mortal bodies. If we were to die without the promise of resurrection, our spirits would forever be bound to the darkness of fallen Lucifer (see verse 8). But because Christ came to this earth, took upon Himself a mortal body, and then voluntarily died and rose again, the bands of death have been forever severed for all who ever inhabit this earth.

The first monster—death—has been defeated. However, another monster—hell—constantly lurks about us through the wiles of the devil, who strives to deceive us, tempt us, and cheat us from everlasting life. This hell, or spiritual death, occurs when our spirits have died to all things good and righteous. That death incrementally attacks us every time we knowingly act contrary to the laws of God. The justifiable demands of a broken law must be met, punishment must be delivered, and mercy must be withheld—if it were not for the all-encompassing suffering and sacrifice of Jesus Christ, which we call the Atonement.

Just as Christ has broken the bands of physical death, He has also broken the bands of spiritual death and holds the keys of mercy for all those who will manifest their faith in His name through repentance and the spiritual cleansing of baptism. As soon as we have entered the kingdom of God through the straight gate (Jesus is the gate and baptism is the key), we are promised that the Holy Spirit will forever be our companion and that we will always retain a remission of our sins if we remember Jesus Christ and keep His commandments. The prophet Moroni teaches the same doctrine: "[T]hey are willing to take upon them the name of thy Son, and always remember him, and keep his commandments which he hath given them, that they may always have his Spirit to be with them. Amen" (Moroni 4:3).

Jacob also describes what happens to those who seek to live according to the ways of the world and the foolishness of men. They will have their reward. In 2 Nephi 9:30–39 is what I call "the sermon for the foolish and wicked," which contrasts with the Sermon on the Mount.

| Sermon on the Mount<br><br>(3 Nephi 12:1–12) | Sermon for the foolish and wicked<br><br>(2 Nephi 9:30–39) |
|---|---|
| 1 Blessed are ye if ye shall give heed unto the words of these twelve whom I have chosen from among you to minister unto you, and to be your servants; and unto them I have given power that they may baptize you with water; and after that ye are baptized with water, behold, I will baptize you with fire and with the Holy Ghost; therefore blessed are ye if ye shall believe in me and be baptized, after that ye have seen me and know that I am.<br><br>2 And again, more blessed are they who shall believe in your words because that ye shall testify that ye have seen me, and that ye know that I am. Yea, blessed are they who shall believe in your words, and come down into the depths of humility and be baptized, for they shall be visited with fire and with the Holy Ghost, and shall receive a remission of their sins. | 30 But wo unto the rich, who are rich as to the things of the world. For because they are rich they despise the poor, and they persecute the meek, and their hearts are upon their treasures; wherefore, their treasure is their god. And behold, their treasure shall perish with them also.<br><br>31 And wo unto the deaf that will not hear; for they shall perish.<br><br>32 Wo unto the blind that will not see; for they shall perish also.<br><br>33 Wo unto the uncircumcised of heart, for a knowledge of their iniquities shall smite them at the last day.<br><br>34 Wo unto the liar, for he shall be thrust down to hell.<br><br>35 Wo unto the murderer who deliberately killeth, for he shall die. |

3 Yea, blessed are the poor in spirit who come unto me, for theirs is the kingdom of heaven.

4 And again, blessed are all they that mourn, for they shall be comforted.

5 And blessed are the meek, for they shall inherit the earth.

6 And blessed are all they who do hunger and thirst after righteousness, for they shall be filled with the Holy Ghost.

7 And blessed are the merciful, for they shall obtain mercy.

8 And blessed are all the pure in heart, for they shall see God.

9 And blessed are all the peacemakers, for they shall be called the children of God.

10 And blessed are all they who are persecuted for my name's sake, for theirs is the kingdom of heaven.

11 And blessed are ye when men shall revile you and persecute, and shall say all manner of evil against you falsely, for my sake;

36 Wo unto them who commit whoredoms, for they shall be thrust down to hell.

37 Yea, wo unto those that worship idols, for the devil of all devils delighteth in them.

38 And, in fine, wo unto all those who die in their sins; for they shall return to God, and behold his face, and remain in their sins.

39 O, my beloved brethren, remember the awfulness in transgressing against that Holy God, and also the awfulness of yielding to the enticings of that cunning one. Remember, to be carnally-minded is death, and to be spiritually-minded is life eternal.

After this point in his discourse, Jacob focuses on the heavy issue of repentance. Now that he has explained the joyous possibilities of salvation for all who penitently turn to God, Jacob anxiously urges his brethren to put aside all forms of idolatry, iniquity, and wickedness, that they might fully partake of the most delicious and pure fruit of the Atonement:

> O, my beloved brethren, turn away from your sins; shake off the chains of him that would bind you fast; come unto that God who is the rock of your salvation.
>
> Prepare your souls for that glorious day when justice shall be administered unto the righteous, even the day of judgment, that ye may not shrink with awful fear; that ye may not remember your awful guilt in perfectness, and be constrained to exclaim: Holy, holy are thy judgments, O Lord God Almighty—but I know my guilt; I transgressed thy law, and my transgressions are mine; and the devil hath obtained me, that I am a prey to his awful misery. (2 Nephi 9:45–46)

Jacob acknowledges that he has spoken hard words of truth against the wicked, but he does so out of love for their souls and out of desire that they might lift up their heads and rejoice in the salvation offered to them through the plan of God:

> O, my beloved brethren, give ear to my words. Remember the greatness of the Holy One of Israel. Do not say that I have spoken hard things against you; for if ye do, ye will revile against the truth; for I have spoken the words of your Maker. I know that the words of truth are hard against all uncleanness; but the righteous fear them not, for they love the truth and are not shaken. . . .
>
> Come, my brethren, every one that thirsteth, come ye to the waters; and he that hath no money, come buy and eat; yea, come buy wine and milk without money and without price.
>
> Wherefore, do not spend money for that which is of no worth, nor your labor for that which cannot satisfy. Hearken

diligently unto me, and remember the words which I have spoken; and come unto the Holy One of Israel, and feast upon that which perisheth not, neither can be corrupted, and let your soul delight in fatness.

Behold, my beloved brethren, remember the words of your God; pray unto him continually by day, and give thanks unto his holy name by night. Let your hearts rejoice. (2 Nephi 9:40, 50–52)

I commend repeated and thorough readings of this beautiful chapter to let the truths wash over and fill your soul.

## 2 Nephi 10—Discourse Conclusion and Revelation of the Name "Christ"

One of the most significant aspects of Jacob's discourse is that for the first time in the Book of Mormon, the title of Christ is used. A careful study of the Book of Mormon chapters before 2 Nephi 10 reveals that Lehi, Nephi, and Jacob use many terms—including Lord, God, and frequently "the Holy One of Israel"—to refer to Jesus Christ. However, in Jacob's concluding discourse, he tells the people through revelation from an angel that God's Anointed would be known as Christ. From this point forward in the Book of Mormon, the name/title Christ is used liberally—more than three hundred times, in fact. Incidentally, the name Jesus is not revealed in the Book of Mormon until 2 Nephi 25, this time to Jacob's older brother Nephi.

We notice in chapter 10 that Jacob is continuing the discourse he began the previous day. After giving his introduction (see 2 Nephi 6), reading two Isaiah chapters (see 2 Nephi 7–8), and giving a lengthy exposition on the doctrines of the plan of salvation (see 2 Nephi 9), Jacob sent everyone home for the evening. It was probably a wise move. Such a discourse would require much spiritual stamina for both preacher and listener. A similar event occurred when Jesus Christ visited the Book of Mormon peoples. After spending a long day teaching and healing, Jesus said to them:

I perceive that ye are weak, that ye cannot understand all my words which I am commanded of the Father to speak unto you at this time.

> Therefore, go ye unto your homes, and ponder upon the things which I have said, and ask of the Father, in my name, that ye may understand, and prepare your minds for the morrow, and I come unto you again. (3 Nephi 17:2–3)

It is a wonderful instructional technique to pause for time to think, ponder, and reflect on the message and then return for a second helping. Our spirits and our minds, like muscles, can only be stretched so far before they need time to relax and heal and strengthen in preparation for more stretching and growth.

Like the other chapters in Jacob's discourse, the key themes and ideas here speak of the gathering work of salvation God will do in the latter days. God will raise up Gentile nations to support and nurse gathering Israel. The American continent will be a land of promise and a land of gathering for many of the house of Israel. Jacob prophesies that the descendants of his people will be remembered at this time and the promises of the ages will be fulfilled unto them:

> For I will fulfil my promises which I have made unto the children of men. . . .
> Wherefore, I will consecrate this land unto thy seed, and them who shall be numbered among thy seed, forever, for the land of their inheritance; for it is a choice land, saith God unto me, above all other lands, wherefore I will have all men that dwell thereon that they shall worship me, saith God. (2 Nephi 10:17, 19)

Jacob concludes his discourse with a burst of encouragement and joy, which ultimately is a defining purpose of his message:

> And now, my beloved brethren, seeing that our merciful God has given us so great knowledge concerning these things, let us remember him, and lay aside our sins, and not hang down our heads, for we are not cast off; nevertheless, we have been driven out of the land of our inheritance; but we have been led to a better land, for the Lord has made the sea our path, and we are upon an isle of the sea. . . .

Therefore, cheer up your hearts, and remember that ye are free to act for yourselves—to choose the way of everlasting death or the way of eternal life.

Wherefore, my beloved brethren, reconcile yourselves to the will of God, and not to the will of the devil and the flesh; and remember, after ye are reconciled unto God, that it is only in and through the grace of God that ye are saved.

Wherefore, may God raise you from death by the power of the resurrection, and also from everlasting death by the power of the atonement, that ye may be received into the eternal kingdom of God, that ye may praise him through grace divine. Amen. (2 Nephi 10:20, 23–25)

Knowing that we are of the house of Israel allows us to liken these verses unto ourselves as well. May we do so and find the joy Jacob expected for those who trust and live his true words.

# REFLECTIONS ON SYMBOLISM IN THE ATONEMENT: INSIGHTS FROM THE BOOK OF MORMON (2 NEPHI 9; JACOB 1–2; MOSIAH 2)[63]

I LOVE THE VARIOUS WAYS words and symbolism can instruct us about the Atonement. For example, I've seen in the scriptures how blood is a symbol of responsibility. The Atonement is inseparable from blood. Therefore, the atoning blood of Jesus Christ can absolve us of the responsibility for our own sins—symbolized by bloody garments—if we repent.

Consider the words of Jacob, King Benjamin, and God, all of whom speak of the symbolic nature of blood on garments representing responsibility and sin. Jacob preached:

> O, my beloved brethren, remember my words. Behold, I take off my garments, and I shake them before you; I pray the God of my salvation that he view me with his all-searching eye; wherefore, ye shall know at the last day, when all men shall be judged of their works, that the God of Israel did witness that I shook your iniquities from my soul, and that I stand with brightness before him, and am rid of your blood. (2 Nephi 9:44)

Jacob used symbolic imagery of blood on garments to describe how the Atonement had saved him from the sins of those over whom he had responsibility because he had faithfully taught the truth. Later, Jacob recorded:

> And we did magnify our office unto the Lord, taking upon us the responsibility, answering the sins of the people upon our own heads if we did not teach them the word of God with all diligence; wherefore, by laboring with our

might their blood might not come upon our garments; otherwise their blood would come upon our garments, and we would not be found spotless at the last day. (Jacob 1:19)

Giving further explanation, Jacob expounded on his priestly responsibilities, again using the symbol of blood:

> Now, my beloved brethren, I, Jacob, according to the responsibility which I am under to God, to magnify mine office with soberness, and that I might rid my garments of your sins, I come up into the temple this day that I might declare unto you the word of God. (Jacob 2:2)

Other Book of Mormon prophets understood that blood is a symbol of responsibility, and they expressed through vivid imagery that the Atonement had washed them clean from the blood (sins) of those over whom they had responsibility. King Benjamin declared:

> I say unto you that I have caused that ye should assemble yourselves together that I might rid my garments of your blood, at this period of time when I am about to go down to my grave, that I might go down in peace, and my immortal spirit may join the choirs above in singing the praises of a just God. (Mosiah 2:28)

In the latter days, God has renewed this blood-cleansing promise to all those who faithfully declare the truth: "And inasmuch as they do this they shall rid their garments, and they shall be spotless before me" (D&C 61:34).

Ironically, the only way to purify our garments from blood and sins is to fully wash our garments in blood, but not in the impure blood of our sins or the sins of this world. Rather, we must completely wash our garments in the blood of Jesus Christ—in other words, we need to take advantage of the Atonement.

If we stand before Jesus Christ in the last day with our garments spotted with our sins or the sins of this world, we stand condemned. On the other hand, if we stand before the Lord with the purifying and cleansing blood of the Lamb covering our garments, effectively erasing our own blood, we have the promise of exaltation in the Lord's kingdom.

The Atonement is real only for those who seek to be spiritually real. In other words, the Atonement has no efficacious power in our lives if we flee from recognizing, confessing, confronting, and overcoming our sins and weaknesses. If we erroneously believe we can save ourselves, we have no need of the Atonement, and hence the Atonement is dead to us; it is not real.

But if in humility we acknowledge our sins, pride, and weaknesses before the Lord and stand courageously to confront them in the power of His almighty Atonement, then we are the most real—the most alive, enlivened, and empowered through the Atonement of Jesus Christ. In Him we are spiritually alive; without Him we are spiritually dead. Only those who recognize their need for the Savior and have enough faith to turn to Him are the ones who are spiritually real and for whom the Atonement is real.

# THE INSTRUCTIVE POWER OF THE SILENCE OF ISAIAH IN THE BOOK OF MORMON[64]

UNDERSTANDING THE WORDS OF ISAIAH is something many aspire to but sometimes find difficult. One basic element of Isaiah's writing is Hebrew poetic parallelism; understanding how this works can make Isaiah's writing style easier to understand.

In the most basic sense, *parallelism* is this: An author expresses an idea (A1). Then the author expresses or reinforces that idea again (A2).

Isaiah 2 is full of parallelism. Parallelism, of which chiasmus may be the most well-known example, is an ancient literary technique of expression.

From this basic pattern, many imaginative derivations can be created. An author can state an idea (A1) but then invert the parallel statement (not A1). Or the author can maximize or minimize the idea (A1). The author can create complex forms of parallelism with multiple elements. Or the author could drive to a central thesis and then return to his starting point, as in chiasmus, which may be the most well-known example of parallelism. The beauty and power of this literary style are found in how the basic pattern is changed, amplified, used—or misused—by the author to make a point.

The authors who skillfully employ parallelism create literary beauty that is both delightful to read and instructive to dissect.

## Examples of Parallelism in the Scriptures

Using Isaiah 2 as found in the Book of Mormon (see 2 Nephi 12), I will provide some representative examples of parallelism, including chiasmus. I use *italics*, <u>underlining</u>, and **bold** formatting to show where Isaiah uses repetition in imagery.

*Example of Simple Parallelism in 2 Nephi 12:2–3 (see also Isaiah 2:2–3):*

And it shall come to pass in the last days, when the mountain of the Lord's house

A1 shall be *established* in the **top** of the mountains,
A2 and shall be *exalted* **above** the hills,
   B1 and **all** *nations* shall flow unto it.
   B2 And **many** *people* shall go and say,
      C1 *Come* **ye**,
      C2 and let **us** *go* up
         D1 to the *mountain* of the Lord,
         D2 to the *house* of the God of Jacob;
            E1 and he will *teach* **us** of his ways,
            E2 and **we** will *walk* in his paths;

*Example of Simple Chiastic Parallelism in 2 Nephi 12:3 (see also Isaiah 2:3):*

A1 for **out** of *Zion*
   B1 shall go forth the <u>law</u>,
   B2 and the <u>word</u> of the Lord
A2 **from** *Jerusalem.*

*Example of Simple Parallelism in 2 Nephi 12:4 (see also Isaiah 2:4):*

A1 And he shall *judge* among the **nations**,
A2 and shall *rebuke* many **people**:
   B1 and they shall beat <u>their swords into plow-shares</u>,
   B2 and <u>their spears into pruning-hooks</u>—

*Example of Extended Alternate Parallelism in 2 Nephi 12:7 (see also Isaiah 2:7):*

A1 Their *land* also is full of **silver and gold**,
   B1 *<u>neither is there any end</u>* of their **treasures**;
A2 *their land* is also full of **horses**,
   B2 *<u>neither is there any end</u>* of their **chariots**.

## Why Parallelism Matters and What It Teaches Us

Significantly, breaking the pattern can be a powerful way to reinforce an overall theme, idea, or doctrine. Just when one has become comfortable with the structure of parallelism, expecting ideas to be repeated in a familiar structure, suddenly the pattern is broken, and we are driven to ask why. It is then that what is missing—the lack of words that we would expect to be there on the page—point to the most significant theme of the entire chapter.

It is silence that speaks loudest in 2 Nephi 2:11 (see also Isaiah 2:11):

A1 The <u>lofty</u> looks of **man** shall be *humbled,*
A2 and the <u>haughtiness</u> of **men** shall be *bowed down,*
    B1 and the **Lord alone** shall be *exalted* in that day.
    B2

So important is the message of God's inimitable exaltedness that Isaiah repeats this parallelistic silence in 2 Nephi 2:17, creating a higher-order parallelism or reflection between these two verses:

A1 And the <u>loftiness</u> of **man** shall be *bowed down,*
A2 and the <u>haughtiness</u> of **men** shall be *made low;*
    B1 and the **Lord alone** shall be *exalted* in that day.
    B2

We would expect a complementary phrase in B2 to say something about the Lord in His exalted status. Instead, nothing occupies that place in the text; we are greeted with silence.

Why?

Isaiah wished to powerfully reinforce that the Lord ***alone*** will be exalted in that day. From a Hebrew parallelistic literary perspective, how do you reinforce the concept that the Lord is ***alone*** in His exaltation? By not even having the Lord share that exalted space with another sentence declaring His exaltation.

Brilliant, beautiful, sophisticated.

With this basic introduction to ancient Hebrew parallelism, you can be empowered to seek and find patterns throughout the writings of Isaiah, other Hebrew prophets, and the Book of Mormon. The effort to find these scriptural literary patterns and structures can enliven your reading and bring enhanced meaning and appreciation of the inspired words of God.[65]

## Jacob 1—Prophetic and Priesthood Responsibility

We owe much to faithful Jacob. He and his direct posterity preserved for us a crucial portion of the Book of Mormon—the small plates of Nephi (1 Nephi through Omni)—which include all the key doctrines and principles of the gospel essential for happiness in this life and eternal life in the hereafter. In Jacob's own words, he describes his zeal to teach and record the truth for his people and their posterity:

> [Nephi] gave me, Jacob, a commandment that I should write upon these plates a few of the things which I considered to be most precious . . . and that I should preserve these plates and hand them down unto my seed, from generation to generation.
>
> And if there were preaching which was sacred, or revelation which was great, or prophesying, that I should engraven the heads of them upon these plates, and touch upon them as much as it were possible, for Christ's sake, and for the sake of our people. (Jacob 1:2–4)

Jacob truly laid up treasures in heaven by making the treasures of the gospel accessible to all. Of all the verses of scripture that speak of faithful Jacob, the one I believe to be most important for understanding his drive for righteousness is Jacob 1:19:

> And we did magnify our office unto the Lord, taking upon us the responsibility, answering the sins of the people upon our

own heads if we did not teach them the word of God with all diligence; wherefore, by laboring with our might their blood might not come upon our garments; otherwise their blood would come upon our garments, and we would not be found spotless at the last day.

If we read Jacob's sermons, writings, scriptural quotations, and scriptural interpretations with this verse in mind, our hearts will be enlightened, enabling us to feel his fervent testimony and commitment to fulfilling his priesthood responsibility to share the message of truth. Perhaps our own testimonies will grow all the brighter as we observe and hear the ways that Jacob sought to "magnify [his] office unto the Lord."

Let's look carefully again at this defining verse for Jacob and learn how we might seek the kingdom of God, following Jacob's example.

One key aspect of Jacob's faithfulness was his commitment *to magnify his God-given responsibilities*. We will see more of this when we read his two-chapter sermon in Jacob 2–3. Jacob understood that part of magnifying his office unto God meant he was responsible for the sins and wickedness of his people *unless* he taught them the truth. In language that we seldom use today, Jacob declared that the blood and sins of his generation would be upon his garments if he did not fulfill his responsibilities with faithfulness.

Is it really true that one person could be held accountable for another's misdeeds? Must one suffer because of the wrongs of another? Will the Lord withhold salvation from a soul because his brother did evil? How can we believe such doctrine? Do not the scriptures verify that "We believe that men will be punished *for their own sins*" (Articles of Faith 1:2; emphasis added)?

It is true that as agents unto ourselves, we are responsible for our own thoughts, words, and deeds. Yet those upon whom the Lord has placed the heavy and solemn mantle of authority *must* preach the truth so that each agent (each one of us) can be put in a state of full choice between truth and error. We are responsible for our own sins only insofar as we have truth, light, and knowledge about the gospel; those who sin in "ignorance" will not be held to such a high standard as those who sin against the light. But before we begin desiring such ignorance to avoid the responsibility of living within the light, let us remember that those who truly are ignorant of the gospel cannot partake freely and fully of the waters of life. The doors of salvation are shut unto them until the voice of gospel gladness is spoken in their ears.

Let's return to the original question: how can one person be responsible for another's sins? Consider this: If the tools of salvation are in the hands of one who does not share with others, how can that tool-bearer-of-salvation justifiably avoid the burden of responsibility for those who fall ignorantly? He cannot. In spiritual terms, the blood of transgression is placed upon the person who had the light and knowledge to share with others but who withheld it from them.

Why do Jacob and other prophets use the metaphor of blood? Blood has always been a symbol of responsibility. To say that the blood of another's sins is upon your garments, then, is to say that you are responsible for the wrongs and evils committed by another because you failed to warn him with the principles of truth. By lifting the warning voice of salvation through faith and repentance, one is cleansed of the staining blood of another's sins through Christ's Atonement.

A similar concept is taught in the New Testament book of James: "Let him know, that he which converteth the sinner from the error of his way shall save a soul from death, and shall hide a multitude of sins" (James 5:20).

Similarly, we hear the promise in Doctrine and Covenants 62:3: "Nevertheless, ye are blessed, for the testimony which ye have borne is recorded in heaven for the angels to look upon; and they rejoice over you, and your sins are forgiven you."

Ultimately, and significantly, only those with pure garments are invited into the kingdom of God.

Though he was reluctant to have to preach such stern admonitions to his people, Jacob well understood this principle—that God promises spiritual cleansing to those who preach the truth. Not only are the stains of others removed from one's garments, but so are one's own stains removed through the blood of Christ. And miraculously, we must stain our garments with the pure blood of Jesus Christ in order that the blood on our garments be purged and removed.

Jacob longed to share healing and consoling words to the pure and the innocent, to lift up the hearts of those who hung down. But understanding his responsibility to make the truth known to his people, he did not shrink from his duty, though it weighed him down with desire and anxiety for the welfare of their souls.

In Jacob 2:4, Jacob confessed that the people had kept the commandments that he had delivered to them. He was free of the responsibility of their guilt. And those who had kept the commandments were also free from blood-stained garments. But the Lord had spoken again to Jacob (see Jacob 1:16–17), requesting that he warn the people of new forms of sin that were besieging their spirits: pride and immorality. If Jacob did not continue to heed the voice of the Lord, warning his people as directed, telling them the reality of truths and the consequences of sins, then he would be spotted with responsibility.

It was a heavy and serious responsibility that Jacob bore. We see in his writings that he felt the weight of his calling:

> Wherefore we labored diligently among our people, that we might persuade them to come unto Christ, and partake of the goodness of God, that they might enter into his rest, lest by any means he should swear in his wrath they should not enter in, as in the provocation in the days of temptation while the children of Israel were in the wilderness.
>
> Wherefore, we would to God that we could persuade all men not to rebel against God, to provoke him to anger, but that all men would believe in Christ, and view his death, and suffer his cross and bear the shame of the world; wherefore, I, Jacob, take it upon me to fulfil the commandment of my brother Nephi. (Jacob 1:7–8)

## Jacob 2—Sermon against Pride and Sexual Immorality

Jacob commenced his sermon by explaining the purposes for preaching to the people: to fulfill his responsibility to God, to rid his garments of the sins of the people, and to preach the word of God (see verse 2). We hear Jacob's anguished voice having to preach so sternly in the presence of the tender, delicate, and chaste in the audience (see Jacob 2:6–9). In particular, the imagery of verse 9 is evocative: *dagger, wound,* and *pierce* contrast with *healing, consoling,* and *delicate.*

Again, the theme of blood and sins is repeated, albeit with different terminology. Jacob used the word *wound* five times in reference to those delicate and tender souls who had suffered because of the sins of others. These tender individuals had come to the temple for healing and consolation, but Jacob lamented that his strong words against sin would be like placing daggers to enlarge the wounds of their souls.

Such stark language of death and dying makes us wonder what manner of terrible wickedness existed. The Nephite atrocities were no different than those in our own day—pride and sexual immorality. Listen to Jacob's words and see how they apply to our own day:

**Pride**

> This land . . . is a land of promise unto you and to your seed, [it] doth abound most plentifully. And the hand of providence hath smiled upon you most pleasingly, that you have obtained many riches; and because some of you have obtained more abundantly than that of your brethren ye are lifted up in the pride of your hearts. (Jacob 2:12–13)

How detestable it would be to use the gifts and riches of God to hurt, oppress, and persecute others, especially those who have not. What wickedness it would be that if instead of supporting the needy with our riches, we turn and persecute them with the very tools of deliverance God has given us.

Jacob pleaded with his people: seek for the kingdom of God before you seek for riches (see Jacob 2:18); do not let pride destroy your souls (see Jacob 2:16); do not think yourselves better than others because you have more abundantly (Jacob 2:13–14); what greater abomination could exist than to persecute another because you have and they do not (see Jacob 2:20–21); and that the purpose of this life is to glorify God, not to seek for riches (2:21). Those riches could be any form of wealth, such as education, learning, power, prestige, accolades, titles, position, money, shelter, opportunities, freedoms, and so on.

Jacob's blistering words did not end there. He spoke of grosser (or greater) crimes that his people were committing. Before we discuss these greater crimes, we must see how the Nephites justified themselves in their wickedness (and we should give the benefit of the doubt that some were acting in ignorance, hence the need for Jacob to teach). Like us, the Nephites had access to scriptures, but they used the scriptures to justify their unrighteous lifestyle and actions. We should pause for self-inventory. Do we ever justify ourselves because of the traditions of our fathers/mothers or because of things written in the scriptures? Just because scriptures record that a prophet was burned at the stake for preaching about Jesus Christ is no justification for us to follow suit. Obviously, we must not imitate every word of scripture that we read, or we risk practicing wickedness.

### Sexual Immorality

The grosser sins of the Nephites that Jacob deplored were those of sexual immorality, specifically infidelity in the marriage relationship. The Nephite men had wounded the souls of their wives and destroyed the confidence of their children because of their bad examples in seeking after wives and concubines outside the bonds of sacred marriage, just as David and Solomon of the Bible had done.

The Lord has spoken plainly:

> [T]here shall not any man among you have save it be one wife. . . .
> I, the Lord God, delight in the chastity of women. . . .
> [T]his people shall keep my commandments [of covenant fidelity] . . . or cursed be the land for their sakes. (Jacob 2:27–29)

## Jacob 3—Words to the Pure and "Filthy"

Having preached the strict word that caused wounds to be enlarged, Jacob turned to words of healing:

> But behold, I, Jacob, would speak unto you that are pure in heart. Look unto God with firmness of mind, and pray unto him with exceeding faith. . .
> O all ye that are pure in heart, lift up your heads and receive the pleasing word of God, and feast upon his love; for ye may, if your minds are firm, forever. (Jacob 3:1–2)

What is significant are the promises to the pure in heart who look unto God:

> Blessed *are* the pure in heart: for they shall see God. (Matthew 5:8)
> But blessed are the poor who are pure in heart, whose hearts are broken, and whose spirits are contrite, for they

shall see the kingdom of God coming in power and great glory unto their deliverance; for the fatness of the earth shall be theirs. (D&C 56:18)

> Yea, and my presence shall be there [the temple], for I will come into it, and all the pure in heart that shall come into it shall see God. (D&C 97:16)

On the opposite end of the spectrum are those who have dark hearts, who are spiritually filthy—filthy because of sin and wickedness. Jacob addressed them again as well. He told them to repent of the false notion that they are somehow more righteous than those they judge to be "physically filthy," as if physical appearance was the measure of spiritual fitness:

> Wherefore, a commandment I give unto you, which is the word of God, that ye revile no more against [the Lamanites who practice marital fidelity] because of the darkness of their skins; neither shall ye revile against them because of their filthiness; but ye shall remember your own filthiness, and remember that their filthiness came because of their fathers. (Jacob 3:9)

Jacob closed his sermon with a rousing call of resurrection from deep spiritual sleep.

## Jacob 4—Knowing and Truth

Ever vigilant in his calling, Jacob opened this new chapter by again citing his responsibility in the ministry. This falls into the pattern established by the thesis statement of Jacob 1:19: "And we did magnify our office unto the Lord . . . laboring with our might."

Chapter 4 is full of Jacob's testimony of Christ and the everlasting Atonement. But it is more than that. It is an exposition on knowing and truth. Without explicitly saying so, Jacob made bold statements to answer such questions as, "What is truth?" and "How do we know the truth?" "How is truth preserved, transmitted, and conveyed?" Just consider some of the rich vocabulary and phrases culled from the verses of this chapter. Ask yourself if they do not lend answers to the questions just posed (whether in the negative or affirmative):

| Word or Phrase | Verse |
|---|---|
| Ministered in word | 1 |
| We know | 1 |
| We write records | 1 |
| Some records perish and vanish | 2 |
| Knowledge | 2 |
| Receive | 3 |
| Look | 3 |
| Learn | 3 |
| We have written | 4 |
| They may know | 4 |
| We knew | 4 |
| Believed in Christ | 5 |
| Search | 6 |
| Revelation | 6 |
| Spirit of prophecy | 6 |
| Hope | 6 |
| Faith unshaken | 6 |
| God showeth us | 7 |
| By his grace and condescensions we know | 7 |
| His mysteries are unsearchable | 8 |
| Impossible to find out all his ways | 8 |
| No man knoweth his ways but by revelation | 8 |
| Despise not revelations | 8 |
| Take counsel from the Lord | 10 |
| He counsels in wisdom | 10 |
| Be reconciled to God | 11 |

| | |
|---|---|
| Attain a perfect knowledge of Christ | 12 |
| Attain knowledge of the resurrection and the world to come | 12 |
| Prophesy to the understanding of men | 13 |
| Spirit speaks the truth | 13 |
| Spirit does not lie | 13 |
| Truth is things are they are, as they will be | 13 |
| Truth is manifested plainly | 13 |
| We are witnesses | 13 |
| Prophets of old are witnesses | 13 |
| Stiffneckedness of Jews | 14 |
| Despised the words of plainness | 14 |
| Killed the prophets | 14 |
| Sought for things they could not understand | 14 |
| Blindness | 14 |
| Looking beyond the mark (brought blindness) | 14 |
| God took away plainness | 14 |
| God gave them things they could not understand | 14 |
| We receive what we desire | 14 |
| Led by spirit of prophesying | 15 |
| Perceive by the workings of the Spirit | 15 |
| Jews will reject the stone of safe foundation | 15 |
| I will unfold this mystery | 18 |

There is one sure way to receive truth and knowledge—revelation! "No man knoweth of [God's] ways save it be revealed unto him; wherefore, brethren, despise not the revelations of God" (Jacob 4:8). If we despise the revelations of God, then we are cut off from all knowledge of God. No amount of thinking or reasoning will reveal God to us. We cannot discover God simply through thinking. No, He must reveal Himself to us, and we must open our hearts to receive. If not, we are in utter darkness concerning the points of truth that lead to eternal happiness and salvation.

God has sent us revelation! There are prophets in our midst today engaging in the cleansing work of preaching truth. We too may know as surely as they, by the spirit of prophecy, that these things are true. And when we do, our garments will be cleansed in Christ as we press forward in faith, hope, and charity making these great things known unto the inhabitants of the earth (see 2 Nephi 2:8).

May we follow the ways of knowing that lead to eternal truth.

# WRESTLING FOR ANSWERS: ENOS, LEHI, AND OTHERS FROM SCRIPTURES WHO ASKED DIFFICULT QUESTIONS[67]

Sometimes I feel I'm the only one who seems to struggle to get answers to prayers. Then, of course, I get corrected by the scriptures. We are not alone in our struggle. Consider the stories of five individuals in scripture, people like you and me, who have also wrestled for answers.

## Enos

Enos is probably the easiest scriptural character to remember as one who struggled for answers. He wrote only a single chapter in the Book of Mormon, and most of that chapter is dedicated to the life-changing event he had with God through prayer.

Enos opens his record telling us, "I will tell you of the wrestle which I had before God, *before* I received a remission of my sins" (Enos 1:2; emphasis added). I highlight the word *before* to emphasize the work that is involved in prayer.

I've always loved the imagery that Enos employed to describe his experience. He depicts that he was out hunting beasts. But who is the real animal he was seeking to slay? He wanted to slay his own fallen nature through the Atonement of Jesus Christ. Just as an arrow would sink deep into the heart of a wild beast to slay it, so too did the words of "eternal life, and the joy of the saints, [sink] deep into [his] heart" (Enos 1:3). Just as he had physically hungered for food, he now hungered for the food of eternal life, the fruit of the Atonement, proclaiming "And my soul hungered" (Enos 1:4).

Enos was intent.

Just as he would have labored all day and night to hunt wild beasts, he instead hunted his own soul: "And I kneeled down before my Maker, and I cried unto him in mighty prayer and supplication for mine own soul; and all the day long did I cry unto him; yea, and when the night came I did still raise my voice high that it reached the heavens" (Enos 1:4).

What did Enos want? And why?

Enos thought he wanted a remission of sins. But in the process of discovering the personalized nature of Christ's Atonement, he was filled with charity, the pure love of Christ, and began desiring that others would taste of the fruit of the Atonement as he had tasted. He prayed for his brethren the Nephites, "[pouring] out [his] whole soul unto God for them. . . . struggling in the spirit" (Enos 1:9–10). Eventually, God promised Enos that He would bless the Nephites insofar as they kept the commandments.

The real test came when Enos felt the pure desire to pray for his enemies, the Lamanites: "I prayed unto [God] with many long strugglings for my brethren, the Lamanites. . . . I . . . prayed and labored with all diligence" (Enos 1:11–12).

For his diligence and faith in wrestling with God for answers, Enos won God's promise to spread the gospel among the Lamanites, that they might also taste of the beauty of Christ's sacrifice and love.

What promises might we gain if we wrestle with God?

*The lesson we learn from Enos: Let your wrestling with God bring salvation to you and others through sincere charity.*

## Hannah

One of the often-overlooked yet beautifully meaningful scripture stories is that of Hannah, the mother of Samuel (see 1 Samuel 1). She was a Sarah figure—barren, hoping to have children that she could teach to follow in the ways of the Lord.

Her righteous desire went unmet for many long decades. Feeling bitter and heartbroken, she went before the Lord at the tabernacle (the precursor to the temple), crying for the Lord to hear her. Eli, the temple priest, seeing her emotional state and murmured prayer, accused her of drunkenness. What a kick in the gut! Right when she had given her whole soul over to God regarding the most tender desire of her heart, someone who should have loved and supported her made false accusations.

Truly the Lord let Hannah wrestle for her answer. She had to contend with divine disappointment and the arrows of fellow fallen-nature humans.

After years of tears, pleading, and patient earnestness, the Lord granted the answer that she desired. Hannah bore Samuel. And true to her word, she dedicated Samuel to the Lord. Samuel grew up at the tabernacle under the tutelage of the high priest Eli and became one of the greatest prophets in all of Israel from the time of Moses to the time of Jesus.

*The lesson we learn from Hannah: Endure in pleading patience for the Lord's answer and be sincere in your promises to God.*

## Gideon

The story of Gideon is unexpected, yet his responses are entirely down-to-earth and human. In Judges 6, we learn that the Midianites were oppressing the Israelites because the Israelites had not been faithful to Jehovah. The angel of the Lord (which may be Jehovah Himself) came to Gideon and told him, "The LORD is with thee, thou mighty man of valour" (Judges 6:12). But Gideon does not immediately respond in a manner we would think is faithful and trusting:

> Oh my Lord, if the LORD be with us, why then is all this befallen us? and where be all his miracles which our fathers told us of, saying, Did not the LORD bring us up from Egypt? but now the LORD hath forsaken us, and delivered us into the hands of the Midianites. (Judges 6:13)

Gideon is human. He's feeling oppressed by the Midianites, wondering where the hand of God is in his life and in the life of his nation, and he justly asks God for clarification.

God takes no offense at the inquisitive, challenging questions Gideon puts to Him: "And the LORD looked upon him, and said, Go in this thy might, and thou shalt save Israel from the hand of the Midianites: have not I sent thee?" (Judges 6:14).

Still wanting to verbally wrestle with God for more confirmation that God will fulfill His promises, Gideon wonders out loud, "Oh my Lord, wherewith shall I save Israel? behold, my family is poor in Manasseh, and I am the least in my father's house" (Judges 6:15).

God tells Gideon again that He will be with Gideon to overthrow the Midianites.

Gideon persists in challenging God, asking, "shew me a sign that thou talkest with me" (Judges 6:17). (Remember that God is appearing to Gideon in the form of an angel, and Gideon is not certain to whom is he is talking.)

To test God, Gideon presents a sacrificial offering. God (acting as an angel) touches it with His staff, causing it to burst into consuming flames. Gideon now believes that he has spoken with God Himself, and he acts on the counsel given him of God.

However, lest we think that Gideon has now achieved some super-human spiritual status, he soon tests God several more times in seeking confirming reassurances that God is truly with him (see Judges 6).

Gideon wrestled with God in a straightforward, honest manner. When Gideon learned through multiple tests of questions to God that God would be faithful to His word, Gideon humbled himself and obeyed the specific directions God had given him. God honored Gideon's faithful doubting, tests, and questions.

*The lesson we learn from Gideon: Challenge and question God when you don't understand or when you need confirmation of His presence; He is faithful and will respond to faithful inquiries.*

## Job

Job's story is both beautiful and perplexing. We may feel inspired to faithfulness like Job, who, having lost all, was still willing to praise the Lord. We may rejoice that all Job lost was not only restored to him but was magnified. We may feel hopeful, too, that in our own suffering, after the trial of our faith, God will restore to us all that we have lost.

For the beauty of how the story of Job ends, we may find ourselves perplexed that God never answered Job's most desperate question: "Why me?" This question, persistently asked by Job throughout his story, is never fully answered, at least not in a way with which many of us feel satisfied. We often want neat, tidy answers that leave no questions, that leave no loose ends, that make everything "happily ever after."

Sometimes there isn't an immediate "happily ever after" in this life. Sometimes God chooses not to answer our prayers, our cries, our wrestling. Sometimes His response to us when we ache with the question "why me?" is what he told Job:

> Where wast thou when I laid the foundations of the earth? declare, if thou hast understanding. . . .
> Hast thou an arm [of strength] like God? or canst thou thunder with a voice like him? . . .

> Canst thou draw out leviathan with an hook? or his
> tongue with a cord which thou lettest down? . . .
> Then Job answered the LORD, and said,
> I know that thou canst do every thing, and that no
> thought can be withholden from thee.
> Who is he that hideth counsel without knowledge?
> therefore have I uttered that I understood not; things too
> wonderful for me, which I knew not. (Job 38:4; 40:9; 41:1;
> 42:1–3)

Translation: Job, I am God! I have my reasons for why everything happens. But I do not owe you an explanation.

You and I are no different. Can we do the acts of God? Can we fully comprehend all of God's works? No.

Job understood his position and his relation to God, and he understood that he may never fully fathom in this life all the reasons for God letting life happen the way it does. Job concluded, "I understood not; things too wonderful for me, which I knew not" (Job 42:3).

*The lesson we learn from Job: Sometimes the answer is that there is no answer—or that we would not understand the answer. Sometimes we must move forward in faith.*

## Lehi

Nephi shares several stories of his father, Lehi, receiving answers to prayer. But the spiritual life for Lehi was not a life of ease. He labored and struggled to have revelation and to be led to the light. Consider Lehi's dream:

> And it came to pass that I saw a man, and he was dressed
> in a white robe; and he came and stood before me.
> And it came to pass that he spake unto me, and bade me
> follow him.
> And it came to pass that as I followed him I beheld my-
> self that I was in a dark and dreary waste. (1 Nephi 8:5–7)

We may be so familiar with the saving grace found in the story of Lehi's dream that we miss this stunning reality: Lehi followed a personage in a white robe who led Lehi into a dark and dreary waste and then left him utterly alone.

*Wait!* you might be thinking. *I thought that if we followed God's servants that we'd find ongoing peace, happiness, and prosperity. How can it be that following God would lead me into suffering, trial, difficulty, despondency, and despair?*

We can learn from Lehi, who pressed forward in faith despite the encroaching and discouraging darkness: "And after I had traveled for the space of many hours in darkness, I began to pray unto the Lord that he would have mercy on me, according to the multitude of his tender mercies" (1 Nephi 8:8).

Though Lehi labored for hours alone, perhaps forgetting about the power of prayer momentarily, when he did remember to pray, Lehi didn't blame God for his trials, didn't shake his fist to heaven and shout "You did this to me!" Instead, Lehi remembered the multitude of the Lord's tender mercies. He let those truths wash over him.

God answered Lehi's prayer and eventually led him to the tree whose beauty is beyond description and whose fruit, which represents the Atonement of Jesus Christ, is the sweetest thing we can ever experience.

*The lesson we learn from Lehi: Know that you must experience the bitter to know and prize the sweet (see D&C 29:39; Moses 6:55).*

## Conclusion

Prayer comes in many forms. Our lives encounter so many varied scenarios. The scriptures provide templates for how to seek after the Lord, how to persist, and how to have faith when we receive—or do not receive—the expected answers to our wrestling. But the reward for patiently wrestling with things we do not understand leads to an increased understanding of God's love and a stronger relationship with Him.

# CHILDREN OF CHRIST: MOSIAH 4–6[68]

COVENANT MAKING AND KEEPING ARE the lifeblood of spiritual living. Covenants teach us of the sacrifice of Jesus Christ. Covenants inspire us to keep the commandments in the name of Christ. And the cords of covenants loose us from the bands of death and hell, sealing us to the everlasting Father and those we love. The speech of the prophet-king Benjamin is one of the most memorable covenant-making scenes in all of scripture.

Reading this passage of scripture helps us see the covenant-making structure of the speech (focusing especially on Mosiah 4–6); the roles of king, people, and God in the covenant-making process; and the doctrinal details that constitute the living power of these covenants.

A covenant is a contract or an agreement between two parties to fulfill specific responsibilities to each other for the purpose of accomplishing some goal. When God covenants with His people (whether as a community or as individuals), the goal is salvation; and the Atonement, coupled with faith and obedience, is the means of that salvation.

## Covenantal Structure of King Benjamin's Speech

Throughout history, God has interacted with His people by means of covenants and covenant making. The Old Testament provides numerous examples of this phenomenon. One of the most salient is the Israelite exodus from Egypt to the covenant-making on mount Sinai:

> In the third month, when the children of Israel were gone forth out of the land of Egypt, the same day came they *into* the wilderness of Sinai.

For they were departed from Rephidim, and were come to the desert of Sinai, and had pitched in the wilderness; and there Israel camped before the mount.

And Moses went up unto God, and the LORD called unto him out of the mountain, saying, Thus shalt thou say to the house of Jacob, and tell the children of Israel;

Ye have seen what I did unto the Egyptians, and *how* I bare you on eagles' wings, and brought you unto myself.

Now therefore, if ye will obey my voice indeed, and keep my covenant, then ye shall be a peculiar treasure unto me above all people: for all the earth is mine:

And ye shall be unto me a kingdom of priests, and an holy nation. These *are* the words which thou shalt speak unto the children of Israel.

And Moses came and called for the elders of the people, and laid before their faces all these words which the LORD commanded him.

And all the people answered together, and said, All that the LORD hath spoken we will do. And Moses returned the words of the people unto the LORD. (Exodus 19:1–8)

Brigham Young University professor Stephen Ricks explained six patterns that are present in ancient Israelite covenant making.[69] This Exodus passage is a prime of example of these patterns, allowing us to see the structure and process of covenant making. Let's break the passage down into its component parts as Ricks relates them:

**Preamble**—"God is introduced as the one making the covenant or in which his prophet is introduced as spokesman for God" (see Exodus 19:3).

**Antecedent history**—"gives a brief review of God's relations with Israel in the past" (see Exodus 19:4).

**Terms of the covenant**—"notes the terms of the covenant, listing specific commandments and obligations that God expected Israel to keep" (see Exodus 19:5–6).

**Formal witness**—"the people bear witness in formal statements that they accept the covenant" (see Exodus 19:8).

**Blessings and curses**—"gives a list of blessings (and curses) for obedience or disobedience to the covenant" (see Exodus 19:5).

**Recital of the covenant and deposit of the text**—"provisions are made for depositing a written copy of the covenant in a safe and sacred place and for reading its contents to the people in the future" (see Exodus 19:7).

Applying these patterns to King Benjamin's speech, the following covenant structure emerges:

**Preamble**—Mosiah 1:1–2:9
**Antecedent history**—Mosiah 2:9–21, 23–30
**Terms of the covenant**—Mosiah 4:4–30 (2:22, 31–41)
**Formal witness**—Mosiah 5:2–8
**Blessings and curses**—Mosiah 5:9–15 (3:24–27)
**Recital of the covenant and deposit of the text**—Mosiah 6:1–3, 6 (2:8, 9)

Because of the significance of the Nephite plea for the Atonement in Mosiah 4:1–3 in response to Benjamin's powerful testimony of Christ, I will add to this list one more pattern—*plea for the covenant and Atonement*. This pattern fits before *terms of the covenant*. Now let's study Mosiah 4–6 with this covenantal structure in mind.

## Plea for the Covenant and Atonement—Mosiah 4:1–3

Mosiah 1–3 set the stage for the covenant, reviewing God's everlasting kindness and mercy toward His people and the state of utter nothingness that we are in before Him. In these early chapters, King Benjamin testified of Jesus Christ, of the fallen nature of mankind, and of our persistent need for His saving Atonement. As soon as Benjamin concluded this portion of his heaven-revealed speech, he observed that his people had fallen to the earth, for "they had viewed themselves in their own carnal state, even less than the dust of the earth" (Mosiah 4:2). The Atonement was the answer, and for this they clamored with broken hearts:

> O have mercy, and apply the atoning blood of Christ that we may receive forgiveness of our sins, and our hearts may be purified; for we believe in Jesus Christ, the Son of God, who created heaven and earth, and all things; who shall come down among the children of men. (Mosiah 4:2)

Benjamin's people requested the atoning blood of Christ that they might have forgiveness and pure hearts. Their supplication was immediately granted.

Verse 3 informs us that "they were filled with joy, having received a remission of their sins, and having peace of conscience" (or purified hearts) because of their faith in Jesus Christ. The Spirit of God had descended on them as in the day of Pentecost (see Acts 2), and they were filled with that unspeakable joy that surpasses all beauty.

Indeed, it is the Spirit of God that conveys the power of the Atonement to our souls, purifies us, and helps us stay clean—or, in other words, to retain a remission of sins. When we have the Spirit of God with us, we are accompanied by a member of the Godhead. Just as members of the Godhead are pure and holy, we likewise become pure and holy when the Spirit is with us. As we keep our covenants and as we remember our Lord and Savior Jesus Christ, the Spirit is with us, just as the sacramental covenant-prayer explains, and we truly have and retain a remission of our sins.

## Terms of the Covenant—Mosiah 4:4–30

Once the people had received the cleansing power of the Atonement and requested the covenant, they were prepared to hear the blessings and responsibilities associated with the covenant. Benjamin renewed his speech by acknowledging that the people's humility had put them in a position where they might truly learn: "God at this time has awakened you to a sense of your nothingness, and your worthless and fallen state" (Mosiah 4:5). Humility is a key ingredient for truly hearing (obeying) the conditions of any covenant.

Let's break this covenant section down into the categories of blessings and responsibilities. The conditions are the means by which blessings from God are obtained, coupled with the grace of Christ.

| Verses | Conditions (Our Responsibilities) | Blessings (God's Responsibilities) |
|---|---|---|
| 6–8 | Come to a knowledge of God's: <br> goodness <br> matchless power <br> wisdom <br> patience <br> long-suffering toward us <br> Atonement <br> Put trust in the Lord <br> Diligently keep the commandments <br> Continue in faith throughout your life | You will find salvation |
| 9–10 | Believe <br> in God <br> that God exists <br> that God created all things <br> that God has all wisdom <br> that God has all power <br> that man does not comprehend all that God comprehends <br> that you must repent of your sins and forsake them <br> Ask in sincerity that He will forgive you <br> Act on what you believe | God will forgive you |

| 11–12 | Remember<br>the joy of receiving remission of your sins<br>the greatness of God<br>your own nothingness<br>God's goodness<br>God's long-suffering<br>Humble yourself<br>Call on the Lord daily<br>Stand steadfast in the faith | You will always rejoice<br>You will be filled with the love of God<br>You will always retain a remission of your sins<br>You will grow in the knowledge of the glory of Him who created you<br>You will grow in the knowledge of what is just and true |

| | | |
|---|---|---|
| **16, 21–28** | Succor (help and support) those who need it<br>Administer your substance to those who need it<br>Do not let beggars ask in vain<br>Do not turn beggars away that they perish<br>Do not withhold your support from those in need because you believe they deserve their lot and position in life<br>Do not judge nor condemn those who have not<br>Impart of your substance to the poor as you are able<br>Feed the hungry<br>Clothe the naked<br>Visit the sick<br>Administer relief temporally and spiritually<br>Do all things in wisdom and order<br>Do not run faster than you have strength<br>Be diligent<br>Return those things that you borrow | You will retain a remission of your sins from day to day<br><br>You will walk guiltless before God |
| **30** | Watch yourselves<br>Watch your thoughts<br>Watch your words<br>Watch your deeds<br>Keep the commandments of God<br>Continue in the faith until the end | You will not perish |

As we can see, God expects much from us, but great are the blessings and rewards. In fact, what we often fail to realize in our mortal state is that God is more eager to bless us than we are eager to receive from His arms of mercy.

Now let's learn from this covenant ceremony. Once the stipulations and responsibilities of each covenant party have been set forth (as Benjamin had thoroughly done), the next step is to receive witness that the covenant has been accepted. Benjamin paused in his speech, "desiring to know of his people if they believed [accepted] the words which he had spoken unto them" (Mosiah 5:1). The people's formal covenantal response follows.

## Formal Witness—Mosiah 5:2–8

And they all cried with one voice, saying: Yea, we believe all the words which thou hast spoken unto us; and also, we know of their surety and truth, because of the Spirit of the Lord Omnipotent, which has wrought a mighty change in us, or in our hearts, that we have no more disposition to do evil, but to do good continually.

And we, ourselves, also, through the infinite goodness of God, and the manifestations of his Spirit, have great views of that which is to come; and were it expedient, we could prophesy of all things.

And it is the faith which we have had on the things which our king has spoken unto us that has brought us to this great knowledge, whereby we do rejoice with such exceedingly great joy.

And we are willing to enter into a covenant with our God to do his will, and to be obedient to his commandments in all things that he shall command us, all the remainder of our days, that we may not bring upon ourselves a never-ending torment, as has been spoken by the angel, that we may not drink out of the cup of the wrath of God. (Mosiah 5:2–5)

Just as Benjamin's people cried out in perfect unity, which is a symbol of the at-one-ment at work, we too in perfect community unity make covenants at the sacrament table and in holy temples. In these instances, we are blessed with power from on high, we are given the promise of Christ's infinite Atonement to cover us as a protective garment, and we witness to God that we will remember His Christ in all that we do, and carry His name with us. Notice the powerful vocabulary of this covenantal response:

- Mighty change in our hearts
- Great views
- Faith that we have
- Great knowledge
- Exceedingly great joy
- We are willing

Ask yourself if these words and phrases describe your own covenant-making experiences.

## Blessings and Curses—Mosiah 5:9–15

Once the people formally entered into a covenant relationship with God, Benjamin proceeded to explain additional blessings for covenant faithfulness as well as the attendant curses that follow infidelity.

Benjamin focused his words on the name of Christ. This is the key word or key name of salvation. When we enter into holy places (the chapel or temple) to make holy covenants, the name by which we make covenants is the name of Christ. And it is by the name of Christ that we are renewed, renamed, and reidentified. It is by the name of Christ that the faithful will be called and will respond in the great and marvelous day of resurrection. This name will endure forever on our souls *if we are faithful*. However, if we turn from the faith, we lose the name of Christ and will be called by some other name, a name that is without salvific power and significance, a name of nothingness.

Let us consider for a moment how significant it is that we have all been renamed by the name of Christ through our covenants. What does *Christ* mean? In its literal translation from the Greek, it means "anointed." Though there is but one Christ, one anointed by the Father to be the Author and Finisher of the work of salvation, all of us can be a christ, an anointed. For example, consecrated olive oil is placed on our heads when we receive blessings. In those moments we are an anointed—we are a christ. Our baptismal and sacramental covenants invite the Atonement to cover and purify us. Truly the blood of Christ anoints our spirits. We are then a christ, an anointed one, anointed in His saving blood, of which olive oil is but a symbol. In our holy temples, we are again anointed in remembrance of Christ's saving love, and again we take His name upon ourselves to signify that like Him, we too are willing to serve in the glorious work of salvation, to act as "saviors on mount Zion" (Obadiah 1:21).

Benjamin exhorts us to keep this name of Christ forever written in our hearts that we may have the blessings of eternal joy:

> Therefore, I would that ye should be steadfast and immovable, always abounding in good works, that Christ, the Lord God Omnipotent, may seal you his, that you may be brought to heaven, that ye may have everlasting salvation and eternal life, through the wisdom, and power, and justice, and mercy of him who created all things, in heaven and in earth, who is God above all. Amen. (Mosiah 5:15)

## Recital of the Covenant and Deposit of the Text—Mosiah 6

Whenever the righteous enter into covenants with the Lord, a record is kept that they might be remembered and nourished in the good word of God:

> And none were received unto baptism save they took upon them the name of Christ, having a determination to serve him to the end.
>
> And after they had been received unto baptism, and were wrought upon and cleansed by the power of the Holy Ghost, they were numbered among the people of the church of Christ; and their names were taken, that they might be remembered and nourished by the good word of God, to keep them in the right way, to keep them continually watchful unto prayer, relying alone upon the merits of Christ, who was the author and the finisher of their faith. (Moroni 6:3–4)

Benjamin did likewise. He "thought it was expedient . . . that he should take the names of all those who had entered into a covenant with God to keep his commandments" (Mosiah 6:1). These names were kept together with the terms of the covenant and shared with appointed priests and teachers so that the people "might hear and know the commandments of God" and remember "the oath which they had made" (Mosiah 6:3).

*Remember!*

This is the key.

*Remember!*

As a learning activity, look for this word and similar words (such as memory, remembrance, and so on) throughout the scriptures. They are everywhere. Our fallen natures are so prone to forgetfulness that a merciful God has generously sprinkled His scriptures with this key word. When we remember Christ, we remember our covenants. When we remember to keep the commandments of God, we will *always* have God's Spirit to be with us. Just think of it! We will have *constant* companionship of a member of the Godhead. When God is with us, we cannot be anything other than holy and pure, for it is the Spirit that purifies and cleanses us by means of the Atonement. And when the Spirit is constantly with us, we have a continual remission of our sins and we are as Christ—clean, pure, and holy. Let us then *remember*!

# MARTYR IN DISGUISE: MOSIAH 12–16[70]

As THE MAN OF GOD returned to the city, most people did not notice him. He had returned to preach the message of repentance that had previously caused this wicked people to seek his life. But this time he "came among them in disguise, that they knew him not" (Mosiah 12:1). In boldness and faith, he stretched forth his hand and announced that he was Abinadi, sent by God to call the people to return to the Lord. The ensuing drama unfolds the most prominent martyr story in the Book of Mormon.

Abinadi's mission was to bear witness to the people of King Noah that unless they repented, they would be afflicted and punished for their sins. Like others with prophetic responsibility, he became a martyr for the cause of God.[71] *Martyr* derives from the Greek language and means "a witness who bears a divine message."[72] Over time, the word took on additional meaning as those who bore divine witness were killed (such as Stephen in Acts 7:55–56). Thus the word *martyr* began to refer to one who was killed for the sake of the witness he bore. Abinadi's story contains significant details that give light to our understanding of the martyr-prophet, the people whom he addressed, and prophetic tradition.

Besides his faithfulness and the words recorded by Alma about Abinadi, almost nothing else is known about Abinadi. Yet his name may reveal information that adds understanding to his persona. Many of the Book of Mormon names are of Hebrew or Egyptian origin. Significantly, when the meaning of a name is brought to light it often seems to fit the plot, character, or detail of the story in which it is found.[73] The name *Abinadi* may be one of those examples. *Abinadi* is possibly formed from two Hebrew words: *abi*, "my father," and *nadi*, "to wander, show grief."[74] Combining these two words may yield the name-phrase "my father wanders" or "my father shows grief."

In essence, Abinadi's name may suggest that he came from a priestly or prophetic class that were "wanderers," perhaps because the wicked did not want to hear their message and so they were cast out of society. Or it may suggest the idea that God the Father shows grief over the wickedness of the people. If these meanings are correct, Abinadi's name contributes to the context of the story while providing additional witness of the divine purpose of his message.

When Abinadi came to Noah's city, he announced himself and began to deliver his prophetic message. When the people cast their attention toward Abinadi, their rage and anger grew as they heard his words of condemnation. Not being able to endure this rude intrusion into their lives, the people seized Abinadi and brought him before King Noah with evil report. King Noah was stirred up to anger by the words of the people. He called in his priests to cross-examine Abinadi in order to find a reason to slay him.

During the questioning period, King Noah's priests demanded that Abinadi explain a passage of scripture. Abinadi retorted, "Are you priests, and pretend to teach this people, and to understand the spirit of prophesying, and yet desire to know of me what these things mean?" (Mosiah 12:25).

Abinadi penetrated further and asked, "What teach ye this people?" (Mosiah 12:27).

In response, the priests replied, "We teach the law of Moses" (Mosiah 12:28). At this response Abinadi wasted no time in systematically displaying the negligence of both priest and king to live or teach the law of Moses.

King Noah reacted in rage and commanded that Abinadi be put to death. As "they stood forth" to "lay their hands on him," he rebuked them, saying he had "not delivered the message which the Lord sent [him] to deliver" (Mosiah 13:2–3). After Abinadi spoke those words, "his face shone with exceeding luster, *even as Moses'* did while in the mount of Sinai . . . and he spake with power and authority from God" (Mosiah 13:5–6; emphasis added).

For the priests of Noah who held Moses in the highest esteem, it is incredible that they were impervious to a prophet who came in the name of the Lord with a face that shone as had Moses's face.[75] If they truly followed Moses, why weren't they willing to follow a prophet who *looked like* and taught like Moses? Unfortunately, even this miraculous witness fell on hard hearts—all except for Alma, of course. They were condemned by their own criteria.

The ensuing horror and sadness of this story is well known. Abinadi was ruthlessly burned to death because he would not deny his witness of the

Lord Jesus Christ. One might ask, why did Abinadi return to the city when he knew that King Noah would seek his life? Even more curiously, why did Abinadi come in disguise and then formally announce himself? Did that formal announcement defeat the purpose of the disguise? No. The disguise was not meant as a protection from harm or danger. Rather the disguise served both a pragmatic and a symbolic purpose.

The pragmatic purpose is that without the disguise, Abinadi would not have been able to enter the city to deliver the message. For the symbolic purpose, the Old Testament affords a comparative story to help explain this "mystery." In 1 Kings 20:35–42, a prophet disguised himself "with ashes on his face" in preparation to deliver a message of divine judgement against King Ahab. In this story, the word *ashes* is better translated as "a covering."[76] Furthermore, it is important to recognize that during this Old Testament time period this type of covering "covered a distinctive mark on the forehead of prophetic guild members."[77] Therefore, it may be that Abinadi's disguise was such that the people did not recognize him to be a prophet.

But what was this distinctive mark? Was it simply "ashes" that symbolized the humiliation and woe of God's judgment upon a wicked people? Or was it the mark of one who had been sealed up to eternal life (see Revelation 22:4)? If the latter, it offers a powerful suggestion as to why Abinadi approached his certain fate with determined courage and faith, saying, "But I finish my message; and then it matters not whither I go, if it so be that I am saved" (Mosiah 13:9).

Abinadi sealed his testimony with his own blood, the most powerful form of testimony, one that cannot be impeached by the passage of time and one that requires the serious reflection and honor of all mankind. Abinadi was a martyr marked on the forehead with the symbol of salvation for his soul and the symbol of destruction for those who rejected his simple message of purity and truth.

# SUFFERING AND SUCCORING IN ALMA 7[78]

WE ALL HAVE DIFFICULT, CHALLENGING, painful experiences in life. Though never pleasant, these experiences can teach us perspective, love, humility, endurance, patience, and, ultimately, how to be more like God.

Consider the story of Abraham and Sarah. These two faithful people endured what seemed like never-ending setbacks and suffering. God sent Abraham away from his homeland to a new promised land. What was the result? Abraham and Sarah discovered a land languishing in famine. Abraham and Sarah moved on to Egypt, only to have Sarah kidnapped. At the very time when God had promised Abraham and Sarah land and posterity (see Genesis 12), they seemed to lose both their promised land and their promised posterity. Why would God challenge and test Abraham and Sarah like this, especially when they had done their best to show diligent obedience to God?

The answer might simply be because they become more Godlike in the striving, in the hoping, in the expecting, in the acting, and ultimately in the receiving of God's good gifts as He fulfilled His promises to them after they faithfully endured suffering and trials.

For some perspective, let's consider the origin of several words. The Latin root word *sub* means "under." The Latin word *fer* means "to carry" (think of words like "ferry" or even "Christofer/Christopher," which means "bearer of Christ"). Thus, the word *suffer* means to be "carried under."

This makes a lot of sense, considering that suffering can metaphorically feel like drowning in difficulty.

The beautiful part of this definition of suffering, however, comes in the antidote: succoring. We read in Alma 7:11–12:

And *he shall go forth, suffering* pains and afflictions and temptations of every kind; and this that the word might be fulfilled which saith he will take upon him the pains and the sicknesses of his people.

And he will take upon him death, that he may loose the bands of death which bind his people; and he will take upon him their infirmities, that his bowels may be filled with mercy, according to the flesh, *that he may know according to the flesh how to succor* his people according to their infirmities. (Emphasis added)

This antidote becomes a powerful message of hope and a symbol of love when we learn that succor means "to run underneath" or to "flow underneath."

In other words, no matter how far you have been *carried under (suffered)*, Jesus has descended below all and He *flows under (succors)* you to support you. At all times. In all places.

God will always be there. Will there be pain? Yes. And sometimes it may seem that each ounce of suffering is another painfully deep scoop from your soul. But it is this depth that allows us to experience a greater depth of Christ's Atonement.

God's love is infinite. He will fill you to fullness. The deeper you've been carved by suffering, the deeper and more profound your love and joy can be. This does not mean we seek out suffering, pain, and difficult experiences; nor does it mean that somehow the pain of suffering is not real because we know that we are gaining God-like depth. It *does* mean that we may not be aware of how much depth we are capable of surviving with God. The stunning reality is that ultimately it is our choice, our radical agency, that determines whether our pain and suffering invite deeper love or result in hardened bitterness.

When we remember that no matter how far under we've been pulled in our drowning suffering, Jesus has descended even further so that He can flow underneath us, run below us, and support us every step of the way as we are carved into the spiritual image of God.

# WHY WAS ABISH ONE OF THE MOST POWERFUL MISSIONARIES IN SCRIPTURE? ALMA 19<sup>79</sup>

WHEN ONE THINKS OF THE heroic missionaries from the Book of Mormon, names such as Ammon, Aaron, Omner, Himni, and Alma the Younger quickly come to mind. We can envision Ammon powerfully defending the flocks of the king and then humbly bearing witness of the gospel. We can hear Alma with a loud voice proclaiming repentance to the people of Ammonihah. Or we can imagine Aaron and his brethren fearlessly heeding the call of the Spirit to teach the king of the Lamanites. Many a modern-day missionary aspires to be like them because

> They had waxed strong in the knowledge of the truth; for they were men of a sound understanding and they had searched the scriptures diligently, that they might know the word of God.
>
> But this is not all; they had given themselves to much prayer, and fasting; therefore they had the spirit of prophecy, and the spirit of revelation, and when they taught, they taught with power and authority of God. (Alma 17:2–3)

With this type of indomitable testimony of the truth, it is no wonder that "they were desirous that salvation should be declared to every creature" (Mosiah 28:3). Yet within the larger picture of the Book of Mormon missionary chapters is a brilliant message of conversion and testimony tucked quietly away between the story of Ammon chopping off Lamanite arms and the miraculous rebirth of Lamoni and his court. It is the unheralded story of Abish in Alma 19.

Several important facts should encourage us to consider Abish more carefully. She is one of only a handful of women who are mentioned by

# WHY WAS ABISH ONE OF THE MOST POWERFUL MISSIONARIES IN SCRIPTURE? ALMA 19[79]

name in the Book of Mormon. Moreover, she is the only Lamanite woman mentioned by name throughout the entire record. Precious few details are given about her life. Nevertheless, we can discern that she was true to the Lord and was zealous in her testimony of Him. This is most clearly attested when, as an exuberant messenger, she ran from house to house proclaiming what the power of God had done for King Lamoni. Why would a seemingly ordinary woman rush to announce the good news? The answer is simple: Faith.

Abish had no ordinary faith. She had the type of faith that Joseph Smith talked about when he said:

> Let us here observe, that three things are necessary in or-
> der that any rational and intelligent being may exercise faith
> in God unto life and salvation. First, the idea that he actually
> exists. Secondly, a *correct* idea of his character, perfections,
> and attributes. Thirdly, an actual knowledge that the course
> of life which he is pursuing is according to his will.[80]

It is this same faith that the heroic Book of Mormon missionaries possessed, and it is clear that they received a correct idea of God's "character, perfections, and attributes" while they diligently searched the scriptures. But how did Abish ever come to this correct knowledge when she was born among a people who rejected the gospel, viciously held to "the traditions of their fathers, which [were] not correct" (Mosiah 1:5), and sought to destroy the faith and gospel records of the Nephites (see Enos 1:14)?

After identifying Abish by name, Mormon reveals a possible solution to this mystery by inserting the editorial comment, "she having been converted unto the Lord for many years, on account of a remarkable vision of her father" (Alma 19:16). Yet even with this further piece of information, we know nothing about the nature of what her father saw, for Mormon makes no further comment about the remarkable vision.

It is often the case throughout scripture that those who saw visions were eyewitnesses of the Lord Himself; see, for example, Lehi's vision in 1 Nephi 1:8–14, Nephi's vision of the tree of life in 1 Nephi 11, Isaiah in Isaiah 6, Moses in Moses 1, and more contemporarily Joseph Smith in Joseph Smith—History 1:15–20. Each of these prophets then testified to the world in faith according to the correct knowledge that they had received of God's attributes.

Might we appropriately see Abish's father fitting into the same pattern? And why not? He gave his daughter a Hebrew name that testified of God's attributes, characteristics he may have come to know in his remarkable vision. *Ab* = father, *ish* = man. In other words, the name *Abish* in Hebrew means "father is a man." Therefore, Abish stands both in name and deed as a witness of one of God's most important attributes—*(God the) Father is a man*.

It is also possible that Abish herself had the vision and learned that God the Father is a man. If so, then her name is an authorial word play that contributes to the meaning and interpretation of the passages.[81]

Abish had missionary zeal because she knew the true attributes of God the Father. It is from this unwavering faith and sure knowledge that she acted with such courageous missionary zeal.

# THE TROPHY OF OUR HEARTS: ALMA 22<sup>82</sup>

DURING THE PASSOVER, JESUS'S LAST meal in mortality, He said to Peter, "I have prayed for thee, that thy faith fail not: and when thou art converted, strengthen thy brethren" (Luke 22:32).

Is conversion something that happens *to* us—something that occurs because of the agency of an outside force? Are we to suppose that Peter was to *wait* until he was converted? To *wait* until some other entity or person exercised agency to make his conversion happen?

What we miss when we read this scripture this way is that *conversion is what we do.* We are the ones who convert ourselves. How does that make sense? Let's look a little more closely into the meaning and history of conversion.

The English word convert means to "fully turn." The underlying Greek word for *convert* used in Luke 22:32 is *epistrepho,* which means "to turn." When Luke uses this verb in his gospel record, the person turning is doing so of his or her own volition and agency. In Luke 2:20, the shepherds "turned themselves" when they returned glorifying. In Luke 8:55, the departed spirit obeyed the voice of God and "turned," or came again to the body, of its own volition. In Luke 17:4, the penitent one chooses to "turn themselves," or repent and return for forgiveness.

This even extends to us. In Luke 17:31, when the day of judgment comes, we are cautioned not to "turn yourself" back to your field, but instead flee to the mountains. In other words, we are the ones making the turn, and fully. If God turns us, then our agency is compromised, our learning is destroyed, and our growth is blighted.

Digging further, we see that the Greek word *epistrepho* is built on the Greek word for *trophy.* What does a trophy have to do with turning and conversion? The word *trophy* means "turning point." This is where things get really interesting.

In the ancient world, when two opposing armies met on the battlefield, eventually one would begin to overpower the other. When that happened, the losing side quickly abandoned all their weapons, protection, and other equipment that might hinder their rapid flight from the battlefield. These losing warriors literally "turned themselves" around and ran. The winning army collected the discarded weapons and equipment, which now served as the symbols—trophies—that they had won the battle!

What *trophies* do we discard so that we might turn ourselves to Jesus? Our sins, our pride, our fears, our careless concerns. Anything that hinders us from turning ourselves to Jesus can be cast down, repented of, and become a token of our willingness to give away anything and everything that keeps us from Jesus.

The Lamanite king of Alma 22 declared his trophies when he said,

> O God, Aaron hath told me that there is a God; and if there is a God, and if thou art God, wilt thou make thyself known unto me, and I will give away all my sins to know thee, and that I may be raised from the dead, and be saved at the last day. (Alma 22:18)

This king was willing to abandon all his sins that he had used to fight against Jesus, that he had used to "shield" himself from Jesus. The king left his sins on the battlefield as "trophies" for Jesus. Once the king had shed these trophies, turning himself to Jesus, God could "conquer" his soul, bringing him to true safety and peace.

Returning to Jesus's statement to Peter, "when thou art converted, strengthen thy brethren," agency is fully in Peter's hands. Peter is the one who must choose to fully turn himself, to give himself over to the Lord and His service. Just like all of us.

Our conversion is our choice. And our actions demonstrate our choice.

Therefore, the trophies of our conversion are a broken heart, a contrite spirit, and a willing mind focused squarely in the direction of Jesus on the battlefield for our soul.

# WHAT DOES GOD THINK OF STRANGERS? WHAT DID THE NEPHITES DO (ALMA 27)? WHAT SHOULD WE DO?[83]

THE CHILDREN OF ISRAEL WERE long oppressed in Egypt as strangers (foreigners) in a strange land. Even their ancestors Abraham and Jacob/Israel were Syrians who had been dispossessed from their homeland. This fact was a regular part of an Israelite testimony, as expressed during solemn worship services of thanksgiving and gratitude to God at the Jerusalem temple: "A Syrian ready to perish was my father, and he went down into Egypt, and sojourned there with a few, and became there a nation, great, mighty, and populous" (Deuteronomy 26:5).

## The Israelites As Strangers

As recounted in the five books of Moses, God rendered mighty acts of wonder to save the children of Israel as strangers in a strange land. He brought His people to Sinai to make a covenant with them that He would be their God and they would be His people. God promised to grant them peace and prosperity in a chosen land if they demonstrated unswerving loyalty to Him.

What was the sign of such unswerving loyalty? Faithful commitment and obedience to the law of Moses that God had given them at Sinai: "Wherefore ye shall do my statutes, and keep my judgments, and do them; and ye shall dwell in the land in safety" (Leviticus 25:18).

Significantly, even after the Israelites received their promised land, God continued to call them *strangers*. Only He truly owned the land. They were strangers and sojourners on the land that God granted them as long as they were loyal to Him as demonstrated by keeping all the laws of God: "The land shall not be sold for ever: for the land is mine; for ye are strangers and sojourners with me" (Leviticus 25:23).

Israelites also long acknowledged that they were but strangers and so-journers in the land God had given them; they knew their safety and security were secured through faithful adherence to all the laws God had established. As the Psalmist wrote, "Hear my prayer, O LORD, and give ear unto my cry; hold not thy peace at my tears: for I am a stranger with thee, and a sojourner, as all my fathers were" (Psalms 39:12).

## The Nephites Taking in Strangers

When God established His covenant with the children of Israel, He gave explicit instructions concerning how they were to demonstrate loyalty to Him, including taking care of widows, orphans, and strangers. Without their covenant loyalty, the children of Israel could not expect the promised blessings and protections offered through God's covenant.

One such example of a branch of Israel keeping this commandment to not oppress the stranger and thus reap the promised blessings was that of the Nephites during their wars with the Lamanites in Alma 27. When the Anti-Nephi-Lehis—Lamanites who had so long terrorized the Nephites—converted to the gospel, the Nephites gave these "strangers" a place to live in the Nephite homeland. The Nephites then used their own strength of arms, even to the point of dying, to protect these Lamanites.

Significantly, the Nephites gave the Lamanite converts a land called *Jershon*, likely a derivation of a Hebrew word that means "place of dwelling for a stranger." For a comparative name, Moses named his firstborn son Gershom: "And [Zipporah] bare [Moses] a son, and he called his name Gershom: for he said, I have been a stranger in a strange land" (Exodus 2:22).

The Nephites welcomed the strangers into their homeland and protected them under the laws and statutes of the law of Moses: "Also thou shalt not oppress a stranger: for ye know the heart of a stranger, seeing ye were strangers in the land of Egypt" (Exodus 23:9).

The Nephites knew that if they betrayed their loyalty to God by not keeping the law of Moses, they could no longer expect the protecting promises of God, which they so desperately needed.

## Why Does God Want Us to Care for Strangers?

Why did God make such explicit commands about protecting strangers, widows, and orphans? Because these individuals are among the most vulnerable of all God's children. That vulnerability was particularly pronounced and acute in the ancient world. God seeks especial care for the most vulnerable on earth, promising His wrath upon those who will not show mercy:

> Thou shalt neither vex a stranger, nor oppress him: for ye were strangers in the land of Egypt.
> Ye shall not afflict any widow, or fatherless child.
> If thou afflict them in any wise, and they cry at all unto me, I will surely hear their cry;
> And my wrath shall wax hot, and I will kill you with the sword; and your wives shall be widows, and your children fatherless. (Exodus 22:21–24)

Later Israelite prophets reminded the people of their duties of covenant loyalty and the attendant promises:

> If ye oppress not the stranger, the fatherless, and the widow, and shed not innocent blood in this place, neither walk after other gods to your hurt:
> Then will I cause you to dwell in this place, in the land that I gave to your fathers, for ever and ever. (Jeremiah 7:6–7)

Unfortunately, as the prophet Zechariah so powerfully described, the ancient Israelites turned away from the security of their God-given covenant:

> Thus speaketh the LORD of hosts, saying, Execute true judgment, and shew mercy and compassions every man to his brother:
> And oppress not the widow, nor the fatherless, the stranger, nor the poor; and let none of you imagine evil against his brother in your heart.
> But they refused to hearken, and pulled away the shoulder, and stopped their ears, that they should not hear.
> Yea, they made their hearts as an adamant stone. . . . (Zechariah 7:9–12)

Because the ancient Israelites, who were strangers on the land God gave them, would not treat other humans with humanity and God-commanded respect, God scattered the Israelites as strangers across the earth:

> But I scattered them with a whirlwind among all the nations whom they knew not. Thus the land was desolate after them, that no man passed through nor returned: for they laid the pleasant land desolate. (Zechariah 7:14)

The implications from scriptures are clear. If we seek peace and prosperity from God—who, as the Creator of this world, owns the land on which we live—then we must be willing to live all His commandments as a sign of our undeviating loyalty to Him. Such loyalty includes treating all God's children with respect, even protecting the stranger (foreigner) and remembering that we ourselves are "strangers" on this earth.

# THE TURNING OF THE NEW YEAR: MORE EVIDENCES FOR THE BOOK OF MORMON— ALMA 51[84]

SOME CHAPTERS AGO WE CONSIDERED a story in the Book of Mormon being set at night as evidence for its ancient authenticity. Let's consider another creeping-by-night story. At the end of chapter 51 in the book of Alma, we hear the story of the Nephite general Teancum going forth at night to seek out Amalickiah, the opposing general in the Lamanite army. Teancum finds the tent of Amalickiah and assassinates him with a javelin. Successfully returning to his camp, Teancum wakes his soldiers and has them stand ready to battle.

What many of us miss, however, are some important details regarding the calendar. They appear at the beginning of the next chapter:

> And now, it came to pass in the twenty and sixth year of the reign of the judges over the people of Nephi, behold, when the Lamanites awoke on the first morning of the first month, behold, they found Amalickiah was dead in his own tent; and they also saw that Teancum was ready to give them battle on that day.
>
> And now, when the Lamanites saw this they were affrighted. . . . (Alma 52:1–2)

Notice that this took place on the first day of the first month—New Year's Day. We know that it was extremely laborious to engrave on the plates, so why would Mormon occupy any space on the plates with dates? And why should we care about the date?

In the ancient Near Eastern culture, which likely influenced Book of Mormon culture, New Year's Day was the time when the king of the land sallied forth to demonstrate his vitality and liveliness, positioning himself to successfully rule as a king for another year. The rising forth of the king on this day was like a divine foreshadowing of a prosperous year. A dead king was the sure sign of a disastrous future.

Hence, no act could be more psychologically demoralizing to an opposing army than to find their king dead on New Year's Day. Teancum chose to assassinate Amalickiah on New Year's Eve. By doing so, he sought to win a massive psychological victory against the Lamanites by sending a message of disaster, despair, and fear.

The seemingly small details in the text of the Book of Mormon matter. In narrative context, they signify the authenticity of the Book of Mormon as an ancient text. Through it all, remember the overall message of the Book of Mormon: that Jesus is the Christ.

# WHAT DOES GOD REALLY MEAN WHEN HE SAYS "BE OF GOOD CHEER"?[85]

In modern-day scripture, God tells His Saints to "be of good cheer":

> Wherefore, be of good cheer, and do not fear, for I the Lord
> am with you, and will stand by you; and ye shall bear record of
> me, even Jesus Christ, that I am the Son of the living God, that
> I was, that I am, and that I am to come. (D&C 68:6)

We live in a world where our senses and our sense of reality are assaulted daily to the point where we might wonder how anyone can be cheerful. So, when God commands us to be of good cheer, does that mean we simply smile and "fake it till we make it," hoping that these tricks will somehow bring us lasting happiness?

Perhaps there is another way.

I believe that we can be of good cheer when we remember who the Lord is and that He is with us.

Consider similar statements from the Old Testament where God tells His people "to be strong and courageous" and be not dismayed:

> Only *be thou strong and very courageous*, that thou may-
> est observe to do according to all the law, which Moses my
> servant commanded thee: turn not from it to the right hand
> or to the left, that thou mayest prosper withersoever thou
> goest . . . .
>
> Have not I commanded thee? *Be strong and of a good
> courage*; be not afraid, neither be thou dismayed: for the
> Lord thy God is with thee whithersoever thou goest . . .

> *Be ye therefore very courageous* to keep and to do all that
> is written in the book of the law of Moses, that ye turn not
> aside therefrom to the right hand or to the left. (Joshua 1:7,
> 9; 23:6; emphasis added)

In the days of Joshua, God prepared His people to conquer the promised land. The people needed to be strong and courageous in order to engage in battle to possess the land.

Such strength came from the Lord. Courage grew as the people remembered that God Himself is the "Lord of Hosts" or the "Lord of *Sabaoth*" (a Hebrew word that means hosts). The phrase "Lord of Hosts" describes God's heavenly powers as the God of the universe who sits in council with heavenly attendants who do His bidding. Some of these heavenly attendants join Him in battle to defeat His enemies. If you are going to do battle, why not fight with the Lord of Hosts at your side instead of relying only on the arm of flesh?

Our battle today isn't a war involving swords and shields and arrows. It is a fight for our time and attention. Will we spend our time on things that are merely amusing, or will we attend to the things that matter most?

When God—the Lord of Heaven and Earth—is with us, we can be strong, courageous, and of good cheer. We see positive examples of this principle in action throughout the scriptures.

In the days of the prophet Elisha, the king of Syria waged war against Israel, encompassing the city where Elisha was, causing Elisha's servant to be deeply fearful. In response, Elisha declared:

> Fear not: for they that be with us are more than they that
> be with them.
> And Elisha prayed, and said, LORD, I pray thee, open his
> eyes, that he may see. And the LORD opened the eyes of the
> young man; and he saw: and, behold, the mountain was full of
> horses and chariots of fire round about Elisha. (2 Kings 6:16–17)

The Lord of Hosts had come with His heavenly hosts to protect His people.

In the Book of Mormon when the Nephites did not keep the commandments of God, they no longer had the protecting power of the Lord of Hosts. In the days of Moronihah, Lehi, and Nephi, the Nephites had grown wicked:

And because of this their great wickedness, and their boastings in their own strength, they were left in their own strength; therefore they did not prosper, but were afflicted and smitten, and driven before the Lamanites, until they had lost possession of almost all their lands. (Helaman 4:13)

The Nephites could not be strong and courageous, for they did not "keep and . . . do all that is written in the book" of God's law (Joshua 23:6). They had lost the presence of God in their lives:

For behold, they saw that the strength of the Lamanites was as great as their strength, even man for man. And thus had they fallen into this great transgression; yea, thus had they become weak, because of their transgression, in the space of not many years. (Helaman 4:26)

How does one become strong? Courageous? Of good cheer?
By keeping all of God's commandments.

Yet how do we press forward when we struggle to find joy despite living righteously? When we experience the realities of depression or the death of a loved one or any other challenges experienced in this fallen state, what is there to be cheerful about?

The strength of the Lord is with us when we make faithful commitment to God a way of life. We must trust that God's promises are sure—that God goes before us, opening the way. We take hold of our covenants made with God, those two-way binding commitments ensured by God, and we place our all on the altar to God. We serve those around us, we act with empathy, we give and forgive with fullness. The Atonement will slowly but surely heal the broken areas of our lives.

When we exercise such faithfulness, the sacramental covenant and promise is in force,

They are willing to take upon them the name of thy Son, and always remember him and keep his commandments which he has given them; that they may *always have his Spirit to be with them*. (D&C 20:77; emphasis added)

If God is always with us, how can we fail?

That is exactly what God promises the faithful who will be strong, courageous, and of good cheer, "for I the Lord am with you, and will stand by you" (D&C 68:6).

# LIKE THE DOG TO HIS VOMIT:
## A REFLECTION ON
## HUMAN UNRIGHTEOUSNESS—3 NEPHI 7[86]

JUST THREE YEARS BEFORE THE coming of Christ to the American continent, secret combinations that opposed faithful prophets proclaiming repentance destroyed the stable Nephite government. Social chaos quickly followed as the society divided into numerous clans and tribes (see 3 Nephi 7). Only six years earlier, the people had enjoyed great peace and prosperity because of their repentance and righteousness. But now only darkness and the most dismal of times awaited them.

Why would a blessed and prosperous people choose this destructive path?

Mormon, the great prophet-historian, insightfully explained the whole situation using symbolic terminology:

> And thus six years had not passed away since the more part of the people had turned from their righteousness, *like the dog to his vomit, or like the sow to her wallowing in the mire.* (3 Nephi 7:8; emphasis added)

This is not a pleasant scene to imagine. Yet Mormon wastes no time describing the people's iniquity, nor does he make apologies for so doing. Mormon's use of this symbolism may derive from ancient Israelite society. For example, in Israel a sow (hog) was an unclean animal. Therefore, according to the Mosaic law, anyone who ate a sow became defiled (see Deuteronomy 14:3–8). Similarly, calling someone a dog in ancient Israel was an insult of the basest sort (see 1 Samuel 17:43; 2 Samuel 16:9), as is the case today in many societies. By comparing them to unclean or base animals, Mormon is labeling the Nephite society as intrinsically unclean and base.

The Book of Mormon employs terms sometimes infrequently found in common speech, such as *mire* and *wallowing*. *Mire* is deep mud that thwarts one's progress; *wallowing* is heavy or clumsy movement often associated with a sow rolling its body in the mire. A sow may *wallow in the mire* after being washed clean, becoming just as dirty as before the cleansing took place (see 2 Peter 2:22). These ideas evoke images of uncleanliness, filth, and repugnance. Not only has Mormon labeled the Nephite society as defiled (unclean), he also pointed out their natural tendency to turn to filthy things after having repented and been washed clean by the Atonement.

Returning to the dog imagery, Mormon made one of his more powerful observations in a simple six-word phrase. Consider for a moment why a dog would ever have need to vomit in the first place. Vomiting is a natural biological defense system or process of protection that the body endures when something harmful or disagreeable has been consumed. The dog likely ate because it was hungry, but he chose poorly, consuming a harmful substance. Even after his body properly reacted to save him by ejecting the harmful substance, the dog was not satisfied. He desired something more revolting than his first meal—the harmful substance mixed with his vomit.

The Nephite society, like the dog, had "hunger pangs" and sought to fill them with the fruits of iniquity. These fruits are entirely unsatisfying, leaving one longing for fulfillment. The Nephites reaped the consequences of their folly by spewing out the wickedness they consumed. The Nephites then turned to even grosser iniquities mixed with the first because their appetite for wickedness could never be satisfied. Thus, they fell headfirst into a dizzying downward spiral of self-destruction "like the dog to his vomit, or like the sow to her wallowing in the mire." With this vivid metaphor, Mormon succinctly captured in parallelistic form the cyclical pattern of wickedness and apostasy that the Nephites repeated throughout their history.

# CHRIST'S VISIT TO THE AMERICAS: 3 NEPHI 17–19[87]

CHRIST'S VISIT TO THE AMERICAS marks the climax of the Book of Mormon when we would expect the greatest of epiphanies, the most illuminating of revelations, and the most marvelous of mysteries to be unfolded. Truly, great epiphanies were displayed as Christ descended from heaven or when the angels came down and ministered to the children. Revelation did pour forth and mysteries were indeed expounded. But on closer examination, we recognize that it was the revelation of the simple truths of the gospel accompanied by clear explanation that comprised the mysteries of the kingdom. Our endeavor today as we study these chapters will be to highlight and explore a few simple principles of the gospel that Christ taught during His American ministry, namely prayer and sacrament.

Christ perceived that the multitude felt overwhelmed by the events of His first day among them when He said, "Behold, my time is at hand" (3 Nephi 17:1). Let's list all that the people had experienced that day:

- Christ descending from heaven
- The calling of twelve disciples
- The preaching of the Sermon at the Temple (following the pattern of the Sermon on the Mount)
- An exposition of the scriptures that explained
  —Christ as the fulfillment of the law of Moses,
  —The descendants of Lehi as the "other sheep,"
  —And the gathering of the Lord's people that would take place in the latter days as taught by Isaiah.

With this in mind, it is easy to understand why Jesus exclaimed, "I perceive that ye are weak, that ye cannot understand all of my words which I am commanded of the Father to speak unto you at this time" (3 Nephi 17:2). So, He commanded the multitude to go to their homes "and ponder upon the things which I have said, and ask of the Father, in my name, that ye may understand" (3 Nephi 17:3). Certainly, the people needed time to consider all they had witnessed and all they had been taught.

But Christ's departure was temporarily delayed because of His compassion toward the people: "Behold, my bowels are fill with compassion towards you" (3 Nephi 17:6). We would say, "my *heart* is filled with compassion." The ancient world, on the other hand, believed that the bowels were the seat of emotions. Christ acted on His compassion by healing all their sick and afflicted because of their great faith. He tarried even longer to have the children brought to Him so that He might bless them.

This echoes a similar event recorded in Matthew 19:13. Before Christ blessed the children, He set an example of how to pray: "he himself also knelt upon the earth; and behold he prayed unto the Father" (3 Nephi 17:15). Kneeling may be the most powerful physical symbol of contrition and humility that we can actively express. In the Hebrew language, "to kneel" and "to bless" come from the same word (*barakh*), which suggests a conceptual connection between the two actions.

After instituting the sacrament (which we will discuss below), Christ issued strong counsel about the purpose and power of prayer: "Verily, verily, I say unto you, ye must watch and pray always, lest ye be tempted by the devil, and ye be led away captive by him" (3 Nephi 18:15). Christ held Himself up as the example, reminding them of how He had prayed among them. He encouraged the multitude to follow His light (see 3 Nephi 18:16). But what is probably the most emphatic reason that Christ gave for prayer is that "Satan desireth to have you, that he may sift you as wheat. *Therefore ye must always pray unto the Father in my name*" (3 Nephi 18:18–19; emphasis added).

Christ also counseled the multitude that they should pray in their families, again reminding them that they were to address the Father in the name of the Son (see 3 Nephi 18:21). We can learn from the Book of Mormon that we are not only to pray to God for the welfare of our families, but we are also to pray for the spiritual well-being of those around us (see 3 Nephi 18:22–23).

After these instructions and others pertaining to the order of sacrament, Christ departed. The people immediately undertook a massive missionary project to proclaim the good news that Christ had appeared and would return the next day. As the messengers went forth, we can hear the ringing words of missionary service:

> Wherefore, how great the importance to make these things known unto the inhabitants of the earth, that they may know that there is no flesh that can dwell in the presence of God, save it be through the merits, and mercy, and grace of the Holy Messiah, who layeth down his life according to the flesh, and taketh it again by the power of the Spirit, that he may bring to pass the resurrection of the dead, being the first that should rise. (2 Nephi 2:8)

As promised, Christ returned the next day. The first thing He did was to reinforce the principles He had taught the day before. He commanded the multitude to kneel and to pray. Then Christ Himself knelt and prayed. We have a marvelous record of what He spoke that can serve to inspire us in our own prayers and teach us how we can pray in greater humility and power.

Before we explore Christ's prayer on that day, let's consider the multitude's description the day before of the power of Christ's prayer:

> The eye hath never seen, neither hath the ear heard, before, so great and marvelous things as we saw and heard Jesus speak unto the Father;
> And no tongue can speak, neither can there be written by any man, neither can the hearts of men conceive so great and marvelous things as we both saw and heard Jesus speak; and no one can conceive of the joy which filled our souls at the time we heard him pray for us unto the Father. (3 Nephi 17:16–17)

We truly are blessed to have Christ's prayers from that day recorded for us.

Let's survey what we can learn from Christ's manner of prayer. First, He bowed Himself to the earth in an act of submission and humility (see 3 Nephi 19:19). He addressed the Father directly and then specifically thanked Him for blessings already bestowed. Christ then asked the Father for a specific blessing; He followed that with specific reasons why He was seeking particular blessings. Finally, Christ clearly had the Father's will in mind. He was seeking to glorify the Father by means of the blessings He asked for because He prayed "that we may be one" (3 Nephi 19:23). This manifests the majestic concept of the "at-one-ment," the state of being as one.

Christ closed His prayer and went to observe His disciples. We are told that His countenance did shine upon them; the disciples were as white as the countenance and garments of Jesus (see 3 Nephi 19:25). Christ had prayed that the Father would bestow the Holy Spirit upon those whom He had chosen. The prayer was answered, and the Holy Spirit descended upon the disciples. They were thereby purified by the power of the Spirit even until they were pure like Christ. We will explore this process more thoroughly in connection to the sacrament.

Christ then prayed a second time. We are taught again the pattern we are to follow (see 3 Nephi 19:27–29). Christ bowed Himself to the earth in an act of submission and humility. He thanked the Father for a specific blessing that had been bestowed. Christ then asked for another specific blessing. And He reasoned with the Father about why He was seeking particular blessings.

Here are a few principles of prayer we can draw from Christ's example:

1. Show humility by kneeling
2. Talk to God as our Father
3. Thank Him for specific blessings
4. Discuss our lives in detail with Him
5. Express and explain our righteous desires
6. Reason with Him
7. Be specific

Now let's turn to the principle of sacrament. Before Christ departed on that glorious first day, He instituted the covenant of the sacrament. He also taught the multitude the gospel principles that accompany the covenant of the sacrament.

He began by asking the disciples to bring bread and wine. Bread is the staple of life and symbolizes the body. Christ is the "bread of life," so it is fitting that the "bread of life" was born in the "house of bread" (the Hebrew name *beth-lehem* literally means "house of bread"). He gave His body so that we might live. Just as the Israelites were sustained for forty years on manna, similarly we are spiritually sustained on the manna of Christ's body.

Wine is the symbol of the precious blood of Christ. Since ancient days, wine has symbolized the lifeblood of the body. In the Old Testament, this notion is expressed when wine is figuratively described as "the blood of grapes" (see Genesis 49:11 and Deuteronomy 32:14). Wine is produced by stamping grapes with the feet with great intensity. Thus we often hear Christ exclaim that He has "trodden the wine press alone" (D&C 76:107). It was He who poured forth the wine of healing by means of His own work. He was both the agent who created the wine of salvation and the wine itself.

We know that God is a God of order. At the same time, when Jesus taught the covenant of sacrament, He also established an orderly system for that covenant to be administered, with disciples properly ordained to officiate in that capacity (see 3 Nephi 18:5). Christ then explained the sublime importance and purpose of the sacrament—*to always remember Him*. The majesty of this covenant is found in the promise, "And if ye do always remember me ye shall have my Spirit to be with you" (3 Nephi 18:7).

It was within the context of teaching about the sacrament that Jesus exhorted the multitude to always pray for their own welfare and for the welfare of those around them. He taught that those for whom they prayed may perhaps repent, come unto Him, and receive the emblems of His body and be saved. In this light we are to invite all to come unto Christ. He has not turned us away. Therefore, we are not to turn others away from feasting at the Lord's supper.

Following is an outline of what Jesus taught about how one can come to the altar-table of the Lord's supper:

1. We are to minister unto those who are not yet worthy.
2. We are to pray to the Father in the name of Jesus Christ for them.
3. Once they have repented and have been baptized, they then will have the flesh and blood of Christ administered to them.
4. If they do not repent, they are not to be numbered among the "sheep."
5. That does not mean such a person is to be cast out. Rather we are to continue to minister to them, for perhaps they may repent and be healed by the Atonement of Jesus Christ.

However, we are to always remember that "ye shall not suffer any one knowingly to partake of my flesh and blood unworthily, when ye shall minister it" (3 Nephi 18:28). President David O. McKay once stated:

> To partake of the sacrament unworthily is to take a step toward spiritual death. No man can be dishonest within himself

without deadening the susceptibility of his spirit. Sin can stun the conscience as a blow on the head can stun the physical senses. He who promises one thing and deliberately fails to keep his word, adds sin to sin. On natural principles such a man "eats and drinks condemnation to his soul." (Conference Report, October 1929, 14–15)

What are some of the ways we can be sure that we are worthy to partake of the sacrament?

1. We need to repent of all our sins.
2. Before going to Church on the Sabbath, consider offering a sincere prayer to the Lord asking that the Spirit confirm to you that you are worthy to partake of the sacrament. By so doing, you will have sure knowledge of where you stand before the Lord and that you are making covenants in righteousness.

Let's end our discussion by bringing together the power of prayer and sacrament, tying these principles together through a brief case study of the spiritual progression of the twelve disciples chosen on the American hemisphere. First, the disciples were chosen out of the world because of their faith. Second, they expressed in prayer their fervent desire that the Holy Ghost be granted to them. Third, they received the Holy Ghost because they believed in Christ and prayed in faith (see 3 Nephi 19:22). Fourth, they were then filled with the purifying power of the Holy Ghost and were cleansed.

The disciples became pure as Christ is pure. This purification is attributed to the purifying effects of the Atonement made possible by the sacrifice of Jesus Christ and mediated to us through the fiery presence of the Holy Spirit. Without the Holy Spirit, we cannot partake of the effects of the Atonement. But when the Holy Spirit is with us, we are purified by its holy presence. Therefore, the sacrament covenant reminds and teaches us that if we *always* remember Christ, we will always have the Spirit to be with us. If we *always* have the Spirit to be with us, we will always have a remission of our sins: We will be pure, white, and spotless as is Christ.

Let us pray that our hearts may be one with God in this righteous desire.

# WHAT DOES IT MEAN THAT MORMON WAS QUICK TO OBSERVE?[88]

MORMON, OUR BELOVED NARRATIVE GUIDE through the Book of Mormon, was described by Ammaron, another record keeper, this way: "I perceive that thou art a sober child, and art quick to observe" (Mormon 1:2).

A typical reading of the word *observe* in this verse, reinforced by other uses of the word *observe* in Mormon chapter 1, causes us to think about Mormon's capacity to studiously take note of and report on the world and people around him—a useful skill for any record keeper, even today.

But there may be an additional meaning behind Ammaron's description of Mormon as one who was "quick to observe."

"Quick to observe" may also mean "quick to listen, quick to heed, quick to keep the commandments, quick to *obey*." When we consider this additional definition of *observe*, we can more deeply appreciate why Ammaron chose Mormon as the next Nephite record keeper. In addition to his ability to carefully see and report on the patterns of behavior in his society, Mormon was quick to hear and obey the word of the Lord.

I'll demonstrate this additional meaning by appealing to the definition of the word observe in the Old Testament, New Testament, and the Doctrine and Covenants.

Consider some of the following:

The Lord saved Israel from Egyptian bondage through mighty acts of wonder, and He expected covenant loyalty in return. As a sign of fidelity to Him, God asked the Israelites to hold solemn feasts or holy days. These holy days memorialized God's saving acts. One of the most important Israelite holy periods was the Feast of Unleavened Bread, commemorating the haste with which the Israelites observed to obey the word of the Lord to flee Egypt (a symbol of sin). So quickly did they observe God's command that there wasn't time for the bread to rise. In memorial of this salvation, God instructed the Israelites:

> Ye shall observe [keep] the feast of unleavened bread; for in this selfsame day have I brought your armies out of the land of Egypt: therefore shall ye observe [keep] this day in your generations by an ordinance for ever. . . .
>
> It is a night to be much *observed* [kept] unto the LORD for bringing them out from the land of Egypt: this is that night of the LORD to be observed [kept] of all the children of Israel in their generations. (Exodus 12:17, 42; emphasis added)

Later, God instructed the Israelites in the wilderness on the actions necessary to maintain the peace and prosperity of the promised land He covenanted to give them. That instruction included keeping the Sabbath day holy:

> My sabbaths ye shall *keep* [observe]: for it is a sign between me and you throughout your generations; that ye may know that I am the LORD that doth sanctify you. . . .
>
> Wherefore the children of Israel shall keep the sabbath, to *observe* [keep] the sabbath throughout their generations, for a perpetual covenant.
>
> It is a sign between me and the children of Israel for ever. (Exodus 31:13, 16–17; emphasis added)

As God continued to instruct the people through Moses, He declared, "Speak unto all the congregation of the children of Israel, and say unto them, Ye shall be holy: for I the LORD your God am holy" (Leviticus 19:2). How were the Israelites to achieve holiness? "Therefore shall ye *observe* [keep, obey] all my statutes, and all my judgments, and do them: I am the LORD" (Leviticus 19:37; emphasis added).

When Moses reviewed the law of God a second time with the Israelites, he reminded them: "Ye shall *observe* [keep, obey] to do therefore as the LORD your God hath commanded you: ye shall not turn aside to the right hand or to the left" (Deuteronomy 5:32; emphasis added).

These few passages from the Old Testament make clear that the word *observe* means "to heed, to obey, to keep the commandments."

We see the same use of *observe* in the New Testament. After Jesus returned from the grave to instruct His disciples again, Jesus concluded:

> All power is given unto me in heaven and in earth.
>
> Go ye therefore, and teach all nations, baptizing them in the name of the Father, and of the Son, and of the Holy Ghost:
>
> Teaching them to *observe* [keep, obey] all things whatsoever I have commanded you: and, lo, I am with you alway, even unto the end of the world. Amen. (Matthew 28:18–20; emphasis added)

Even in the last dispensation, God once again uses the word *observe* to convey the sense of obedience and commandment keeping: "And they shall *observe* [keep, obey] the covenants and church articles to do them, and these shall be their teachings, as they shall be directed by the Spirit" (D&C 42:13; emphasis added).

What does this mean about Mormon? Was Mormon truly quick to obey the Lord? To heed His counsel? Let's consider a few passages to reinforce the truth that Mormon was an obedient servant of the Lord—that he was "quick to observe."

- "And I, Mormon, being a descendant of Nephi, (and my father's name was Mormon) I remembered the things which Ammaron commanded me" (Mormon 1:5).

- "And I did endeavor to preach unto this people, but my mouth was shut, and I was forbidden that I should preach unto them; for behold they had wilfully rebelled against their God; and the beloved disciples were taken away out of the land, because of their iniquity. But I did remain among them, but I was forbidden to preach unto them, because of the hardness of their hearts; and because of the hardness of their hearts the land was cursed for their sake" (Mormon 1:16–17).

- "And it came to pass that the Lord did say unto me: Cry unto this people—Repent ye, and come unto me, and be ye baptized, and build up again my church, and ye shall be spared. And I did cry unto this people" (Mormon 3:2–3).

- "I did even as the Lord had commanded me; and I did stand as an idle witness to manifest unto the world the things which I saw and heard, according to the manifestations of the Spirit which had testified of things to come" (Mormon 3:16).
- "Therefore I write a small abridgment, daring not to give a full account of the things which I have seen, because of the commandment which I have received" (Mormon 5:9).
- "Now these things are written unto the remnant of the house of Jacob; and they are written after this manner, because it is known of God that wickedness will not bring them forth unto them; and they are to be hid up unto the Lord that they may come forth in his own due time. And this is the commandment which I have received" (Mormon 5:12–13).
- "Having been commanded of the Lord that I should not suffer the records which had been handed down by our fathers, which were sacred, to fall into the hands of the Lamanites, (for the Lamanites would destroy them) therefore I made this record out of the plates of Nephi, and hid up in the hill Cumorah all the records which had been entrusted to me by the hand of the Lord, save it were these few plates which I gave unto my son Moroni" (Mormon 6:6).

These scriptures demonstrate a consistent characteristic about Mormon: that he sought the will of the Lord and was "quick to observe," to be obedient to the commands of the Lord. Mormon was like faithful Nephi, who was also quick to observe:

> I will go and do the things which the Lord hath commanded, for I know that the Lord giveth no commandments unto the children of men, save he shall prepare a way for them that they may accomplish the thing which he commandeth them. (1 Nephi 3:7)

The next time we read that Mormon was "quick to observe," let us re-member that Ammaron was praising Mormon for taking note of the people and the world around him and that he was diligently heeding and quickly obeying the commandments of God.

May we be like the great record keeper Mormon—to quickly observe, keep, and obey all the words of the Lord.

# I WRITE THAT YE MIGHT BELIEVE THE GOSPEL OF JESUS CHRIST: MORMON 1–9[89]

AFTER PASSING THROUGH NINE HUNDRED years of Book of Mormon history, we arrive at the days of Mormon—a time of great inequality, political insecurity, great wickedness, and marvelous prophecies. Within the small book that bears his name we have the opportunity to explore the life of our religious mentor and historical guide, a man who lived during the final scenes of the last dispensation of the Nephite world. As we venture into these chapters we may feel as ancient Saints once did when they heard the story of another people:

> For they knew not what to think; for when they beheld those that had been delivered out of bondage they were filled with exceedingly great joy.
> And again, when they thought of their brethren who had been slain by the Lamanites they were filled with sorrow, and even shed many tears of sorrow. (Mosiah 25:8–9)

Let's first illustrate Mormon based on the details gleaned from the Book of Mormon. Our appreciation of the Book of Mormon and the doctrinal principles contained therein will increase as we know the prophet who compiled the book. After discussing the characteristics of the prophet Mormon, we will turn to a few of the themes encountered in his short book.

In the first chapter, Mormon describes himself as one who was "learned somewhat after the manner of the learning of my people" (Mormon 1:2). This scribal introduction is similar to what Nephi wrote about himself at the beginning of the Book of Mormon: "I was taught somewhat in all the learning of my father" (1 Nephi 1:1).

Because we do not have a complete knowledge of the manner of learning among the people of Nephi, we cannot make any firm conclusions about Mormon's training as a scribe. Nevertheless, we do know other important characteristics about Mormon. Ammaron, who was likely more than 125 years old when he commissioned Mormon as a keeper of sacred records, stated that Mormon was "a sober child, and . . . quick to observe" (Mormon 1:2). We should clarify the significance of the word *sober*, since so often in our society that word is associated with alcohol. One who is sober is thoughtful, calm, temperate, and moderate. All these characteristics were foundational for Mormon's balanced life as a military general and prophet-historian.

Mormon records that his father, also named Mormon, carried him "into the land southward, even to the land of Zarahemla" (Mormon 1:6). Zarahemla bordered the lands of the Lamanites and was an area of constant friction where the seeds of war were sown. It is possible that Mormon the elder was a military commander (or the chief military commander) who led the Nephites in defense of their homeland against the Lamanites.

If Mormon the elder was a military commander (or the chief military commander), that may explain why Mormon was appointed to be the chief captain of the armies at such a young age—he was only sixteen years old! Mormon may have taken over his father's position when his father died. We hear nothing more of Mormon the elder after the first chapter, which may indicate that he was dead before Mormon the younger became chief commander in the second chapter. This phenomenon may be comparable to Alexander the Great (356–323 BC), who became the general of the Greek armies at the age of twenty when his father, who was the previous general, died.

Returning to chapter one, Mormon displays that he is "quick to observe" when he records that "wickedness did prevail upon the face of the whole land . . . there were no gifts from the Lord, and the Holy Ghost did not come upon any, *because of their wickedness and unbelief*" (Mormon 1:13–14; emphasis added). Despite the general state of wickedness among the people, Mormon kept himself pure and clean before the Lord so that "being fifteen years of age and being somewhat of a sober mind . . . I was visited of the Lord, and tasted and knew of the goodness of Jesus" (Mormon 1:15).

This verse is ripe with significant details and parallels. First, the use of the word taste to describe the Atonement of Jesus Christ is found throughout the Book of Mormon.[90] For example, Lehi describes the fruit of the tree of life as the "most sweet, above all that I ever before tasted" (1 Nephi 8:11).

Another significant detail is that Mormon was fifteen years of age when the Lord visited him. This is similar to what we find in the account of Joseph Smith, who recorded in his history, "I was at this time in my fifteenth year . . . when the light rested upon me [and] I saw two Personages . . . One of them spake unto me, calling me by name and said, pointing to the other—*This is my Beloved Son. Hear Him*!" (Joseph Smith—History 1:7, 17). Mormon concludes chapter one with observations that prophecies of the holy prophets were being fulfilled. Clearly Mormon understood the ancient prophets and prophecies and was in tune with the Spirit to recognize their fulfillment.

Continuing with our description of the man Mormon, we learn that he "was large in stature" despite "being young" (Mormon 2:1). We can compare this to Nephi, who declared:

> And it came to pass that I, Nephi, *being exceedingly young, nevertheless being large in stature*, and also having great desires to know of the mysteries of God, wherefore I did cry unto the Lord; and behold he did visit me, and did soften my heart that I did believe all the words which had been spoke by my father. (1 Nephi 2:16; emphasis added)[91]

Again we notice the similarities between Mormon and Nephi in their personal descriptions:
- Young
- Large in stature
- Somewhat learned
- Have been visited by the Lord

We should not fail to mention that Mormon was a descendant of Nephi (see Mormon 1:5).

As Mormon grew in years, he also grew in the way in which he defined himself. We find Mormon's simple yet powerful testimony embedded in 3 Nephi 5, where he carefully explains the task of being a prophet-historian together with personal details that define who he is. This invaluable description invites us into the heart and mind of the man Mormon. I am going to quote at length from Mormon's own words in 3 Nephi 5 and highlight a few significant passages along the way so that we can discuss in greater detail what manner of man Mormon was:

I have made my record of these things according to the record of Nephi, which was engraven on the plates which were called the plates of Nephi.

And behold, I do make the record on plates which I have made with mine own hands.

And behold, *I am called Mormon, being called after the land of Mormon,* the land in which Alma did establish the church among the people, yea, the first church which was established among them after their transgression.

*Behold, I am a disciple of Jesus Christ, the Son of God.* I have been called of him to declare his word among his people, that they might have everlasting life.

And it hath become expedient that I, according to the will of God, that the prayers of those who have gone hence, who were the holy ones, should be fulfilled according to their faith, should make a record of these things which have been done—

Yea, a small record of that which hath taken place from the time that Lehi left Jerusalem, even down until the present time.

Therefore I do make my record from the accounts which have been given by those who were before me, until the commencement of my day;

And then I do make a record of the things which I have seen with mine own eyes.

*And I know the record which I make to be a just and a true record*; nevertheless there are many things which, according to our language, we are not able to write.

And now I make an end of my saying, which is of myself, and proceed to give my account of the things which have been before me.

I am Mormon, and a pure descendant of Lehi. *I have reason to bless my God and my Savior Jesus Christ, that he brought our fathers out of the land of Jerusalem,* (and no one knew it save it were himself and those whom he brought out of that land) *and that he hath given me and my people so much knowledge unto the salvation of our souls.* (3 Nephi 5:10–20; emphasis added)

There is a wealth of information contained in these verses. I have highlighted some but not all the significant passages so that our religious mentor may be more fully known.

We first notice that Mormon was "called after the land of Mormon." For later generations of the faithful, including Mormon and his family, the land of Mormon may have represented a garden of peace where the love and Spirit of the Lord were in abundance. The land of Mormon may have been esteemed as a most sacred site of reverence, much like our temple sites today. Those who were lovers of peace and those who eschewed war may have longed for the days of tranquility "near the waters of Mormon; yea, the place of Mormon . . . the forest of Mormon, [for] how beautiful are they to the eyes of them who there came to the knowledge of their Redeemer" (Mosiah 18:30). We can almost hear Mormon's voice of longing for that sacred site of peace expressed in this verse as he struggled with the present reality of wickedness rampant in his nation. Might it be that Mormon's own name was synonymous with peace and the knowledge of the Redeemer that was found in the land of Mormon? If so, the sad irony is that Mormon did not live a life of peace, but rather, as he states, "a continual scene of wickedness and abominations has been before mine eyes ever since I have been sufficient to behold the ways of man . . . and my heart did sorrow because of this the great calamity of my people, because of their wickedness and their abominations" (Mormon 2:18, 27).

Another significant insight about the character of Mormon is expressed in the declaration, "Behold, I am a disciple of Jesus Christ, the Son of God" (3 Nephi 5:13). After telling us his name and the origin of that name, Mormon's very next self-definition was that of a disciple of Jesus Christ. Mormon does not state that he was a powerful and successful military leader. He does not boast of his singular opportunity to be a member of a sacred genealogy of record keepers stretching back to the origins of Nephite civilizations. Mormon does not extol himself as a prophet or religious historian. Rather, Mormon states in powerful simplicity that he is a disciple of Jesus Christ, the Son of God. It is with this statement that Mormon defines who he is. He was a man with an eye single to the glory of God.

Later Mormon testifies, "I know the record which I make to be a just and a true record" (3 Nephi 5:18). "And behold, I do make the record on plates which I have made with mine own hands" (3 Nephi 5:11). Again, we can cite the example of Nephi, the originator of Nephite record keeping, who stated in his opening chapter, "I know that the record which I make is true; and I make it with my own hand" (1 Nephi 1:3). Mormon understood his commission to testify of Jesus Christ. He made the record himself and thus knew of his honesty and faithfulness in recording both the gospel and the things that he saw and heard. His son Moroni had the same conviction: "And I exhort you to remember these things; *for the time speedily cometh that ye shall know that I lie not*" (Moroni 10:27; emphasis added).

We learn from the Book of Mormon that Mormon was a man of great gratitude. In the midst of unending wickedness coupled with the near assurance of the complete annihilation of his people whom he loved, Mormon declared, "I have reason to bless my God and my Savior Jesus Christ, that he brought our fathers out of the land of Jerusalem . . . and that he hath given me and my people so much knowledge unto the salvation of our souls" (3 Nephi 5:20). He was not like his compatriots, who would "curse God, and wish to die. Nevertheless they would struggle with the sword for their lives" (Mormon 2:14). Mormon had a righteous perspective; his eye was single to the glory of God despite the adversity of life.

Now that we have a deeper understanding of the man Mormon, let's explore a few key messages that he bore in his own book. I suggest that we study two reoccurring themes: First, "how could ye have departed from the ways of the Lord" (Mormon 6:17); and second, "therefore I write unto you, Gentiles, and also unto you, house of Israel" (Mormon 3:17).

As a historian, Mormon was well acquainted with the iniquity of mankind and the cycle of wickedness. His larger work, which we call the Book of Mormon, records these episodic patterns repeatedly. However, now Mormon records in his own book the events from his day and not those from the distant past. Thus we see that he was a living witness to the very patterns he had so often brought to our attention, that we "may learn to be more wise than [they] have been" (Mormon 9:31).

Mormon's was an era of great iniquity, which led to constant contention and wars. No more than eight verses into his book, Mormon records that war breaks out among the Nephites and Lamanites. Mormon was merely eleven years old at this time, and sadly it was at least sixty-two years before Mormon no longer had to observe "such an awful scene of blood and carnage as was laid before [his] eyes" (Mormon 5:8). His people "were once a delightsome people, and they had Christ for their shepherd; yea, they were led even by God the Father. But now, behold, they are led about by Satan, even as chaff is driven before the wind" (Mormon 5:17–18).

Why, we may ask, would they turn from the Lord? Why would a delightsome and wholesome people turn to such barbarous acts of cruelty and live their lives by the sword? Mormon gives us several answers. He tells us in one passage that, "the Spirit of the Lord hath already ceased to strive with [them]" (Mormon 5:16). In another passage, Mormon states that "they did not come unto Jesus with broken hearts and contrite spirits" (Mormon 2:14). Mormon also records the pride of the Nephites who "had sworn by all that had been forbidden them by our Lord and Savior Jesus Christ, that they would . . . avenge themselves of the blood of their brethren" (Mormon 3:14).

Later Mormon bemoaned, "how can a people like this, whose delight is in so much abomination—How can we expect that God will stay his hand in judgement . . . ?" (Moroni 9:13–14). Despite the hopeless situation, he still preached the message of salvation, "laboring with them continually" (Moroni 9:4), but his people hardened their hearts against the Lord. In the final analysis, Mormon declares the cause of their turning from the Lord: "Behold, the pride of this nation . . . hath proven their destruction" (Moroni 8:27).

As Mormon laments the seemingly unavoidable fate of his people, he interjects many prophecies concerning the coming forth of the Book of Mormon coupled with warnings to those who are to receive this record:

> Now these things are written unto the remnant of the house of Jacob . . . and behold, they shall go unto the unbelieving of the Jews; and for this intent shall they go—that they may be persuaded that Jesus is the Christ, the Son of the living God . . .
>
> And also that the seed of this people may more fully believe his gospel, which shall go forth unto them from the Gentiles. . . .
>
> And also the Lord will remember the prayers of the righteous, which have been put up unto him for them.
>
> And then, O ye Gentiles, how can ye stand before the power of God, except ye shall repent and turn from your evil ways?
>
> Know ye not that ye are in the hands of God? Know ye not that he hath all power, and at his great command the earth shall be rolled together as a scroll?

> Therefore, repent ye, and humble yourselves before him, lest he shall come out in justice against you—lest a remnant of the seed of Jacob shall go forth among you as a lion, and tear you in pieces, and there is none to deliver. (Mormon 5:12, 14–15, 21–24)

We can bring our study to an end with the reminder that Mormon was fully aware that his record was not for his fallen people but for future generations—for us:

> I know that such will sorrow for the calamity of the house of Israel; yea, they will sorrow for the destruction of this people; they will sorrow that this people had not repented that they might have been clasped in the arms of Jesus. (Mormon 5:11)

> Therefore I write unto you, Gentiles, and also unto you, house of Israel. . . .
> Yea, behold, I write unto all the ends of the earth; yea, unto you, twelve tribes of Israel. . . .
> I write unto you all. And for this cause I write unto you, that ye may know that ye must all stand before the judgment-seat of Christ, yea, every soul who belongs to the whole human family of Adam; and ye must stand to be judged of your works, whether they be good or evil;
> And also that ye may believe the gospel of Jesus Christ, which ye shall have among you. . . .
> And I would that I could persuade all ye ends of the earth to repent and prepare to stand before the judgment-seat of Christ. (Mormon 3:17–22)

May we have reason to bless our God and our Savior Jesus Christ that this record has been preserved for our day. May we humbly heed the gospel principles that we may remain in the ways of the Lord. And may we express sincere gratitude to the Lord God for the life and testimony of the prophet Mormon.

# DOES SUFFERING MAKE US BITTER OR BETTER? INSIGHTS FROM THE BOOK OF MORMON AND OTHER SACRED SCRIPTURES[92]

LIFE CAN BE SO UNEXPECTEDLY difficult at times. Yet, because of this, *we must choose to become better, not bitter.*

We may find ourselves perplexed and bewildered by the challenges, difficulties, and suffering that encompass us. Sometimes, we may feel to ask as Joseph Smith and Habakkuk of old asked, "O God, where art thou?" (D&C 121:1; see also Habakkuk 1:2–4). Even Jesus Christ cried out from the depths of His humiliating suffering, "My God, my God, why hast thou forsaken me?" (Matthew 27:46).

In these terrible moments of grueling, exhausting suffering we might ask: Why, if I am keeping the commandments, should I suffer? Why, if I am seeking with all my heart to love God and to love my neighbor, should thorns and hedges block my path? Why does it feel that there is no balm in Gilead? Why do my prayers seem to hit an impenetrable brass ceiling? Why have my friends fled? Why do my enemies prowl about me? Why do I not find solace as I seek the Lord?

These and many other piercing, penetrating questions may flow from our hearts in our deepest distress.

Through it all, we must realize that not one trial is wasted.

All these things are meant to bring us experience and to draw us closer to God, that our love may be fuller, purer, more refined. Our suffering brings empathy and perspective so that we can say without guile, as did Mormon of the Nephites who would not hear the word of God,

> Behold, I . . . had loved them, according to the love of God which was in me, with all my heart; and my soul had been poured out in prayer unto my God all the day long for them. . . .

I fear not what man can do; for perfect love casteth out all fear.

And I am filled with charity, which is everlasting love. (Mormon 3:12; Moroni 8:16–17)

As Apostle Orson F. Whitney testified:

No pain that we suffer, no trial that we experience is wasted. It ministers to our education, to the development of such qualities as patience, faith, fortitude and humility. All that we suffer and all that we endure, especially when we endure it patiently, builds up our characters, purifies our hearts, expands our souls, and makes us more tender and charitable, more worthy to be called the children of God... and it is through sorrow and suffering, toil and tribulation, that we gain the education that we come here to acquire and which will make us more like our Father and Mother in heaven.[93]

How is it possible to feel joy in the midst of such suffering?
We are strong in Christ.
That is the power of the Atonement—it makes us better instead of bitter.
When we are truly at one with God, we are strong in Christ. We leave aside the natural man and we put off the arm of flesh that tempts us to "save" ourselves from suffering. When our hearts have been fully given over to the Lord, the deepest cracks of our brokenness are filled with the warm, saving wax of the Atonement that makes us like new again. Love no longer leaks out of us. We receive love until it overflows, and we share freely with others whose vessels need the purity of love in their lives.

When we are healed by the balm of God, instead of allowing our trials to make us cynical and faithless, they make us stronger and more faithful. The suffering, challenges, heartaches, and difficulties of life become purifying and refining experiences. We love more fully. We enjoy more deeply. We understand more comprehensively. Our patience stretches into the eternities, seemingly, and we know a peace that surpasses all understanding—that pure love of God that pervades His created order.

## How Scriptural Sacrifices Connect to Today's Sacrament[94]

Readers of the Old Testament and the Book of Mormon are often puzzled, if not baffled, at the focus on animal sacrifice. Why kill animals? The Pearl of Great Price may provide the most relevant and beautiful explanation: "This thing is a similitude of the sacrifice of the Only Begotten of the Father, which is full of grace and truth" (Moses 5:7).

Here is context from the ancient world for how sacrifice was understood, but let's start in the modern world.

Our Westernized modern world is carnivorous. We are voracious meat-eaters. Yet, most people today are totally cut off from the realities of meat production.

I'll say it simply: something must die for us to live.

Any time we eat plants or animals, something died to sustain us. Death, ultimately, is a natural part of life—or, at least, in the sustaining of life. But again, most people are entirely cut off from and likely unfamiliar with the process of raising animals, killing them, and preparing their bodies for consumption. Because we have industrialized the process of meat production, very few of us raise animals and then kill them for our evening meal.

The ancient Old Testament and Book of Mormon times were different. People were closer to the process of meat production and consumption. People typically lived with the animals they would eventually eat.

The ancient Old Testament and Book of Mormon times were also different in how people approached killing animals and eating them. Killing animals was a ritualized, sacred activity to be shared in a community; it culminated in a feast attended by family, priests, and God. Instead of the sterile and industrialized killing of animals in our modern food processing, in ancient times the act of killing an animal was prescribed in ritualistic order and detail.

Portions of the animal were consumed by the priest (as payment for his services), a portion was consumed by the individual or family offering the sacrifice, and a portion was consumed by God via the smoke that ascended to heaven from the sacrifice. The purpose of eating this sacred meal together was to strengthen the community, to reinforce the truth that life is sustained by death, to remember that the Lamb of God would eventually give life to all through His death, and to renew the covenantal commitments of the community. Truly, this was a sacred, communal meal.

Although we are no longer required to make animal sacrifices, the meaning is retained today. Consider the weekly sacred meal that we call the sacrament, or the act of making something sacred.

This symbolic meal represents the flesh and blood of Jesus Christ. In turn, the sacrifice of His flesh and blood meant that the flesh and blood of animals were no longer required elements of the sacred meal that brought priest, people, and God together into holy communion. Now we celebrate this communal feast quite simply—at least it appears simple from an outward perspective.

Notice that at our weekly reenactment of the Last Supper, three parties are in attendance. First, the people have gathered together—often in families—petitioning for God's presence and grace. Second, the priests are there to officiate in the ritual and to mediate the experience. Analogously to ancient priests, modern priesthood holders prepare the "flesh and blood" of the holy meal. Finally, and most importantly, God joins the holy meal, communing with His supplicating people.

Remember the words of the sacrament prayer, uttered in humility and precision by the representative priesthood holder:

> O God, the Eternal Father, we ask thee in the name of thy Son, Jesus Christ, to bless and sanctify this bread to the souls of all those who partake of it; that they may eat in remembrance of the body of thy Son, and witness unto thee, O God, the Eternal Father, that they are willing to take upon them the name of thy Son, and always remember him, and keep his commandments which he hath given them, that they may always have his Spirit to be with them. Amen. (Moroni 4:3; see also D&C 20:77)

The last phrase of this oft-quoted verse has long struck me: "that they may always have his Spirit to be with them." If people always remember Jesus Christ, the Lamb of God, the ultimate sacrifice of flesh and blood, then they have the promise that God's presence will always be with them.

Think of that. If God's presence is always with a person, he or she will always retain a remission of sins. Because God cannot dwell in unholy temples, as we remember Jesus Christ we are continuously accessing the never-ending Atonement to become clean and pure so that the presence of God can attend our lives.

Just as individuals and families in ancient times needed a priest to prepare and bless their sacred meals, meals that pointed minds toward the Lamb of God who sustains all life, so too, in the modern day, people gather as individuals and families for priesthood holders to prepare and bless the weekly sacred meal that renews our memory of Christ's sacrifice and our covenant with God.

# THE SURPRISING STORY OF A BOOK OF MORMON IN THE HARVARD LIBRARY<sup>95</sup>

THE BOOK OF MORMON IS the most literarily beautiful, doctrinally truthful, and everlastingly applicable book I've ever encountered.

I've read a lot of books over the years.

During one six-month period in graduate school, I read one hundred densely packed scholarly books and nearly that many more articles on biblical studies and related topics. And during the year 2018, I read more than four hundred and fifty books! I had no idea that the human brain could consume so much incredible content! (You can see the full list of books I've read at taylorhalverson.com.)

Over the average holiday break, I'm known to plow through a dozen books or more.

My wife and I own several thousand books, and we have individually or collectively read nearly every book on our shelves.

I love learning; digging into a book can be one of the most rewarding learning experiences. With a book you may access a lifetime of others' learning and experience, structured and condensed into the most meaningful, accessible and applicable parts.

Even though I have enjoyed thousands of books in my lifetime, many of them providing truly incredible experiences, the Book of Mormon still remains the most literarily beautiful, doctrinally truthful, and everlastingly applicable book I've ever read.

How would you expect this book to be regarded in one of the most important libraries in the world?

The following incredible story about an unusual copy of the Book of Mormon at the Harvard University library was shared with me by Paul Alan

Cox, who is an ethnobotanist and conservationist based in Jackson Hole, Wyoming. Paul gave his permission to share his story below.

In 1978 when I was studying for my doctorate, I spent a lot of time in Widener Library searching obscure literature on tropical rain forest ecology. The Widener Library, which is at Harvard, is second in America only to the Library of Congress in terms of number of volumes, and it is a wonderful resource for scholarly studies.

After a long day of working in the library, I decided to take a break to see if they had any books about my church. The librarian at the reference desk kindly gave me the call numbers. I went up the elevator and into the shelves. I was amazed by the number of books, both pro and con, on the shelves about The Church of Jesus Christ of Latter-day Saints. A small, dusty volume on an upper shelf caught my eye, and I pulled it down.

To my amazement, I found that it was an early edition of the Book of Mormon. When I looked at the front pages, I saw that it was inscribed as a "Gift to Harvard College" by "Brigham Young, of the City of the Great Salt Lake."

Excited by this find, I went back down the elevator to the reference desk to see if I could check the book out. I wanted to show Brigham Young's gift of the Book of Mormon to my wife, Barbara, and our two small children, Emily and Paul Matthew. The librarian told me that I could indeed check out the book, but when she went to stamp the due date at the back of the book, she stopped. "There is no circulation paper here. I will have to glue one in."

When she returned, I asked her if that meant that the book had never been checked out. "Correct," she said, "this book has never been circulated."

She stamped the book. I exited the massive front doors of the Widener Library and descended the long stone steps. I crossed Harvard yard toward my small graduate student office in the basement of the Biological Laboratories, passing en route some of the world's most advanced and expensive laboratories. I thought of the 130 years that this copy of the Book of Mormon I carried had sat on the library shelves untouched, collecting dust, until a young Mormon student finally saw it.

As I thought of the extraordinary truth of the Book of Mormon and the impact that it has had on my life and that of my family, Paul's prophecy to Timothy came to my mind: in the last days people would be "ever learning, and never able to come to the knowledge of the truth" (2 Timothy 3:7).

No matter how many books I read for my doctorate program, or how many volumes are in my personal library, or how many titles I add to the collection of books I've read, Paul Alan Cox's story reminds me to never neglect the one most important book.

I conclude simply. May the Book of Mormon and its unfailing message be ever in our lives.

# FORGIVENESS IS TO ABANDON ALL HOPE OF A BETTER PAST AND WHY THAT BUILDS A BETTER FUTURE: THE FALL OF THE NEPHITE CIVILIZATION[96]

FORGIVENESS IS FUNDAMENTAL TO PERSONAL peace and happiness. Forgiveness is fundamental to civilization.

For many years, I taught two exciting, university-level world civilization courses entitled "History of Creativity in the Arts, Science, and Technology" that covered the dawn of civilization to the present day. I also helped write and edit the two books that accompanied the course.[97]

This "History of Creativity" course helped learners see acts of civilization as acts of creativity. Everything that has brought humanity to where we are today were acts of creativity.

The course also empowered learners to rediscover and act on their own God-given creativity. Learners remembered that one of God's greatest attributes is as a creator. As sons and daughters of God, we partake of His divine capacity for creativity.

President Dieter F. Uchtdorf taught this principle compellingly when he said,

> Remember that you are spirit daughters of the most creative Being in the universe. Isn't it remarkable to think that your very spirits are fashioned by an endlessly creative and eternally compassionate God? Think about it—your spirit body is a masterpiece, created with a beauty, function, and capacity beyond imagination . . . . The more you trust and rely upon the Spirit, the greater your capacity to create.[98]

Of course, learning about the past is not all rosy creativity.

A review of the past invites some trauma and pain. There is much in the collective human past that is terrible, ugly, destructive, unjust, and ungodly.

As we remember the past and as we learn about the past, we might experience feelings of anger or disgust at the actions or inactions of others. We might feel hopeless about the good that has been squandered or lost; we might ache over the broken hearts of God's children that were not gently loved and lifted.

What might soothe such trouble?

It is a principle that I believe we must all embrace in order to come to peace with all pasts, including our own.

When I teach about the past, I also teach the principle of forgiveness: *Forgiveness is abandoning hope for a better past.*[99]

Reflect on that statement.

How many of us wish for different pasts in our lives? How often do we wish to retrieve harsh words spoken that are like seeds of noxious weeds scattered to the wind? How often have we sorrowed over actions made against family or friends that fill us with regret? How often do we consider inaction that has left us wondering "what if"?

Have we ever encountered knowledge about past Church history that leaves us wondering or that creates questions or that leaves us wishing that portions of that past had been different?

Do we ever ache at the fall of the Jaredite or Nephite nations and wonder how their lives and civilizations would have been different had they heeded the words of Jesus?

> Will ye not now return unto me, and repent of your sins, and be converted, that I may heal you?
>
> Yea, verily I say unto you, if ye will come unto me ye shall have eternal life. Behold, mine arm of mercy is extended towards you, and whosoever will come, him will I receive; and blessed are those who come unto me. (3 Nephi 9:13–14)

If we ruminate for too long on the past, we may lose our sense of balance, of peace, and of hope.

We can wish for a better past or we can abandon all hope for a better past, embracing forgiveness that heals the cracks and breaches of unfulfilled expectations.

How do we act on such forgiveness?

- Frankly acknowledge the source of our pain.
- When we feel tempted to remember the past with anger or disillusionment, choose to remember that Christ can make all things whole.
- Express gratitude for the goodness, light, and truth that animates our lives.
- Do not dwell on the pains of the past any longer than is instructive to empower our lives to be better.
- Remember and believe the words of Moroni:

> Condemn me not because of mine imperfection, neither my father, because of his imperfection, neither them who have written before him; but rather give thanks unto God that he hath made manifest unto you our imperfections, that ye may learn to be more wise than we have been. (Mormon 9:31)

As we forgive our own past, we will develop greater empathy, enabling us to forgive the pasts of others.

As we trust in the all-encompassing and all-healing power of Jesus, we will have the strength to abandon all hope of better pasts.

# CONCLUSION

I HOPE THAT SOMETHING I have written has opened your heart and mind to feel and see truths of the Book of Mormon. I hope you feel inspired and empowered to explore the Book of Mormon again, and more deeply—to find and apply truths to your life that will bring you peace, perspective, joy, and love. Like the many authors in the Book of Mormon who labored in faith and humility despite their weakness in writing, I hope you have felt drawn closer to Jesus Christ.

I conclude with my simple testimony of the Book of Mormon, a testimony I hope you have felt and seen stirringly and thoroughly in the pages of this book:

**The Book of Mormon is the most literarily beautiful, doctrinally truthful, and everlastingly applicable book in the world.**

# ENDNOTES

1. This chapter was originally published on LDSLiving.com and is republished with permission.

2. For additional insights on that topic, see Taylor Halverson, "The Kingdoms of Glory," at https://interpreterfoundation.org/the-kingdoms-of-glory-d-131-13219-24-137/.

3. This chapter was originally published as "How the Hebrew Translation of 'God' and 'Jehovah' Might Change Your Understanding of Deity" on LDSLiving.com at http://www.ldsliving.com/How-the-Hebrew-Translations-of-God-and-Jehovah-Might-Change-Your-Understanding-of-Deity/s/86425 and is republished with permission.

4. This chapter is a reworking of several articles that were originally published on LDSLiving.com and are republished with permission.

5. See John Gee, "Four Suggestions on the Origin of the Name Nephi," in *Pressing Forward with the Book of Mormon*, FARMS, 1999, 1–3.

6. Matthew Bowen and Pedro Olavarria, "Place of Crushing: The Literary Function of Heshlon in Ether 13:25–31," *Interpreter: A Journal of Latter-day Saint Faith and Scholarship*, 14 (2015), 227–239; see especially p. 235.

7. For more on the beauty and significance of wordplays in the Book of Mormon, see the Book of Mormon Onomasticon project at Brigham Young University, https://onoma.lib.byu.edu/index.php/Main_Page, and writings of Matthew Bowen at https://www.mormoninterpreter.com/author/matthewb/.

8. This chapter was originally published on LDSLiving.com and is republished with permission.

9. Mark Twain, *Roughing It* (Hartford, CT: American Publishing Co., 1901), 133.

10. Originally published as Taylor Halverson, "Deuteronomy 17:14–20 as a Guide to Book of Mormon Kingship," *Interpreter: A Journal of Latter-day Saint Faith and Scholarship*, 17 (2017), 1–10. Republished with permission.

11. Much has been written about kingship in the Bible. An exhaustive bibliography here is unwarranted, though several recent or relevant reads include Shawn Flynn, *YHWH Is King: The Development of Divine Kingship in Israel* (Leiden, Netherlands: Brill, 2014); David T. Lamb, *Righteous Jehu and his Evil Heirs: The Deuteronomists Negative Perspective on Dynastic Succession* (Oxford, 2005); Jamie A. Grant, *The King as Exemplar: The Function of Deuteronomy's Kingship Law in the Shaping of the Book of Psalms* (SBL, 2004).

12, Daniel I. Block, "The Burden of Leadership: The Mosaic Paradigm of Kingship (Deuteronomy 17:14–20)," *Bibliotheca Sacra* 162 (2005), 259–278; Karl W. Weyde, "The Narrative of King Solomon and the Law of the King: On the Relationship between 1 Kings 3–11 and Deuteronomy 17:14–20," *Enigmas and Images: Studies in Honor of Tryggve N. D. Mettinger*, ed. Göran Eidevall and Blazenka Scheuer (Winona Lake, IN: Eisenbrauns, 2011), 75–91.

13. Much has been written on Book of Mormon kingship. Here are a few pieces to begin with: Todd R. Kerr, "Ancient Aspects of Nephite Kingship in the Book of Mormon," *Journal of Book of Mormon Studies* 1/1 (1992), 85–118; Gordon C. Thomasson, "Mosiah: The Complex Symbolism and Symbolic Complex of Kingship in the Book of Mormon," *Journal of Book of Mormon Studies* 2/1 (1993), 21–38; Val Larsen, "Killing Laban: The Birth of Sovereignty in the Nephite Constitutional Order," *Journal of Book of Mormon Studies* 16/1 (2007), 26–41, 84–85; Stephen D. Ricks, "Kingship, Coronation, and Covenant in Mosiah 1–6," in *King Benjamin's Speech: "That Ye May Learn Wisdom,"* ed. John W. Welch and Stephen D. Ricks (Provo, UT: FARMS, 1998), 233–275.

14. "The Hebrew verb *RBH [to multiply, used in Deuteronomy 17:17] has the nuance of growing exponentially, not just lineally, with respect to something (cf. the same form of the verb used in Deuteronomy 17:16–17 in Exodus 1:10, 12; Deuteronomy 8:13[x2]; Psalms 49:17; Proverbs 29:16; Isaiah 40:29; 55:7; Daniel 11:39; Hosea 12:2)." Ed. W. VanGemeren, (1997). *New International Dictionary of Old Testament Theology & Exegesis* (Vol. 3, 1038–1039). Grand Rapids, MI: Zondervan Publishing House."

15. The same question of "Who is to be king?" dominates and influences significant portions of the Hebrew Bible and not just the narrative sections. The question and potential answers to "Who is to be king?" shows up in the Pentateuch (*Torah*), Prophets (*Nevi'im*), and the Writings (*Ketuvim*).

16. Due to the way I formatted the tables, a challenge arose in seeking to provide a representative scripture for each element of the Deuteronomy 17:14–20

pattern for each Nephite leader discussed. In some instances, the lack of a scripture is taken as evidence for the pattern. For example, there are no scriptures that show Nephi seeking silver and gold for personal gain. Therefore, I do not have a scripture to demonstrate the pattern element "Don't seek after silver and gold."

17. Some examples of scriptures expressing the divine warrior theme include: Exodus 15: 1–7; 2 Samuel 22; Psalms 18; Habakkuk 3. A representative scholarly work on the divine warrior motif in scripture is Charlie Trimm, *YHWH Fights for Them! The Divine Warrior in the Exodus Narrative* (Gorgias Press: Piscataway, NJ, 2014).

18. Robert Boylan applied this approach to Jacob: "Deuteronomy 17:14–20 seems to be the scriptural basis of much of Jacob's comments in Jacob 1–3. For instance, the screed on polygyny seems to be informed by Deuteronomy 17:17 regarding David and Solomon having 'many' wives and concubines (Jacob 2:24)."

19. This chapter was originally published on DeseretNews.com and is republished with permission.

20. More on this topic can be found in Brant Gardner, "Nephi as Scribe," *Mormon Studies Review 23:1, 45–55.*

21. Originally published as Taylor Halverson, "Reading 1 Nephi with Wisdom," *Interpreter: A Journal of Latter-day Saint Faith and Scholarship*, 22 (2016), 279–293. Republished with permission.

22. Useful secondary readings on the ancient Near Eastern Wisdom tradition and literature with specific emphasis on the Hebrew Bible include: Bernard Lang, *Wisdom and the Book of Proverbs: A Hebrew Goddess Redefined* (New York: Pilgrim, 1986); Stuart Weeks, *Early Israelite Wisdom* (Oxford: Clarendon, 1994); Leo G. Perdue, *Wisdom and Creation: The Theology of Wisdom Literature* (Nashville TN: Abingdon Press, 1994); Claus Westermann, *The Roots of Wisdom: The Oldest Proverbs of Israel and Other Peoples*, trans. J. Daryl Charles (Louisville, KY: Westminster/John Knox, 1995); G. I. Davies, "Were There Schools in Ancient Israel?" *Wisdom in Ancient Israel: Essays in Honour of J. A. Emerton*, eds. John Day, Robert Gordon, and H. G. M. Williamson (Cambridge: Cambridge University Press, 1995), 199–211; Michael V. Fox, *Proverbs 1–9: A New Translation with Introduction and Commentary* (New York: Doubleday, 2000); Roland E. Murphy, *The Tree of Life: An Exploration of Biblical Wisdom Literature*, 3rd ed. (Grand Rapids MI: Eerdmans, 2002); James L. Crenshaw, *Old Testament Wisdom: An Introduction*, 3rd ed. (Louisville KY: Westminster/John Knox Press, 2010).

23. Joshua Michael Sears, "'We Came Out from Jerusalem': The Holy City's Influence on Book of Mormon Peoples," *Selections from the Religious*

*Education Student Symposium 2007* (Provo, UT: Religious Studies Center, Brigham Young University, 2007), 130–146, footnote 3; Steven L. Olsen, "The Centrality of Nephi's Vision" in *Religious Educator* 11, no. 2 (2010), 51–66, footnote 1.

24. James L. Crenshaw, *Education in Ancient Israel: Across the Deadening Silence*, The Anchor Bible Reference Library (New York: Doubleday, 1998); Noel B. Reynolds, "Nephi's Teachings in the Book of Mormon" (Transcript, n.d.). Reynolds acknowledges that "Nephi brought all that Jewish education and culture with him to the Promised Land" and later qualifies that as Hebrew literary devices.

25. If, as some scholars suggest, the Bible was the product of scribal schools, then we should look more carefully at what role scribal training and the Wisdom tradition (which often went hand in hand) had in the production of the Book of Mormon. See K. van der Toorn, *Scribal Culture and the Making of the Hebrew Bible* (Cambridge, MA: Harvard University Press, 2007); van der Toorn's work has been criticized by John Van Seters, "The Role of the Scribe in the Making of the Hebrew Bible," *Journal of Ancient Near Eastern Religions* 8/1 (2008), 99–129. For a useful introductory piece exploring Nephi's potential skill and training as a scribe, including implications for interpreting Nephi's writings, see Brant A. Gardner, "Nephi as Scribe," *Mormon Studies Review* 23/1 (2011), 44–55.

26. Even Neo-Assyrian King Ashurbanipal, whose name means "the god Ashur is the creator of the heir," was not originally intended for the throne, being the third son. Instead of being groomed for the throne, he was trained in the scribal arts, within which he appears to have flourished. Indeed, the greatest library of ancient Mesopotamia was assembled at the Assyrian capital of Nineveh by Ashurbanipal due to his love of learning. Incidentally, Ashurbanipal's older brother, Shamash-shum-ukin, was so resentful that his younger brother became the king that he rebelled against him—a rebellion that divided the kingdom in war. Shamash-shum-ukin perished in the fire that destroyed his Babylonian palace, ending the war around 646 BC. Might Laman and Lemuel, not so far historically removed from the significant international events of the Assyrian civil war, have seen Nephi as an Ashurbanipal character—a younger brother trained as a scribe but chosen by the father to be the king—who displaces the legitimate older brothers as rulers and as king; and they wage ruthless war on him? For an article arguing for the scribal training and capabilities of Ashurbanipal, a younger son, see Alasdair Livingstone, "Ashurbanipal: Literate or Not?" *Zeitschrift für Assyriologie und Vorderasiatische Archäologie* 97/1 (2007), 98–118.

27. Laurie E. Pearce, "The Scribes and Scholars of Ancient Mesopotamia," in *Civilizations of the Ancient Near East, Volume IV*, ed. Jack M. Sasson (London: Hendrickson Publishers, 2006), 2265–2278 (especially p. 2270).

28. Books of the Old Testament that are classed as Wisdom literature typically include Proverbs, Job, Ecclesiastes, and, depending on the scholar, also the Song of Solomon and Psalms. It is unlikely that the books we have today would be identical to what Nephi had access to during his scribal training in the Wisdom tradition.

29. John W. Welch, "Chiasmus in the Book of Mormon," in *Book of Mormon Authorship: New Light on Ancient Origins*, ed. Noel B. Reynolds (Provo, UT: Religious Studies Center, Brigham Young University, 1982), 33–52; Matthew Nickerson, "Nephi's Psalm: 2 Nephi 4:16–35 in the Light of Form-Critical Analysis," *Journal of Book of Mormon Studies* 6/2 (1997), 2642.

30. Immanuel M. Casanowicz, *Paronomasia in the Old Testament* (Boston: Norwood Press, 1894); Frank Zimmermann, "Folk Etymology of Biblical Names," in *Volume du Congrès: Genève, 1965* (*Vetus Testamentum Supplement* 15; Leiden, Netherlands: Brill, 1966), 311–326; Herbert Marks, "Biblical Naming and Poetic Etymology," *Journal of Biblical Literature* 114/1 (1995), 21–42; Russell T. Cherry III, *Paronomasia and Proper Names in the Old Testament: Rhetorical Function and Literary Effect*, Dissertation (Louisville, KY: The Southern Baptist Theological Seminary, 1988); Moshe Garsiel, *Biblical Names: A Literary Study of Midrashic Derivations and Puns*, (Ramat Gan, Israel: Bar-Ilan University Press, 1991); Moshe Garsiel, "Puns upon Names as a Literary Device in 1 Kings 1–2," *Biblica* 72 (1991), 379–386; Edward L. Greenstein, "Wordplays, Hebrew," in *The Anchor Bible Dictionary* (New Haven, CT: Yale University Press, 1992), 6:968–971; Moshe Garsiel, "Homiletic Name-Derivations as a Literary Device in the Gideon Narrative: Judges VI–VIII," *Vetus Testamentum* 43 (1993), 302–317. Paronomasia also appears throughout the Book of Mormon.

31. John A. Tvedtnes, "The Hebrew Background of the Book of Mormon," in *Rediscovering the Book of Mormon*, eds. John L. Sorenson and Melvin J. Thorne (Salt Lake City and Provo, UT: Deseret Book and FARMS, 1991), 77–91; S. Kent Brown and Terrence L. Szink, "Lehi," *Encyclopedia of Mormonism* (New York: Macmillan, 1992); Sidney B. Sperry, "The Book of Mormon as Translation English," *Journal of Book of Mormon Studies* 4/1 (1995), 209–217; John A. Tvedtnes and Stephen D. Ricks, "Notes and Communications: Jewish and Other Semitic Texts Written in Egyptian Characters," *Journal of Book of Mormon Studies* 5/2 (1996), 156–163; John Gee, "The Wrong Type of Book," in *Echoes and Evidences of the Book of Mormon*, eds. Donald W. Parry, Daniel C. Peterson, and John W. Welch (Provo, UT: FARMS, 2002), 307–329;

Stephen D. Ricks, "Converging Paths: Language and Cultural Notes on the Ancient Near East," in *Echoes and Evidences of the Book of Mormon*, eds. Donald W. Parry, Daniel C. Peterson, and John W. Welch (Provo, UT: FARMS, 2002), 389–419; D. Jeffrey Meldrum and Trent D. Stephens, "Who Are the Children of Lehi?" *Journal of Book of Mormon Studies* 12/1 (2003), 38–51, 116; John S. Thompson, "Lehi and Egypt," in *Glimpses of Lehi's Jerusalem*, eds. John W. Welch, David R. Seely, Jo Ann H. Seely (Provo, UT: FARMS, 2004), 259–276.

32. Although this chapter focuses primarily on a few themes found in the book of Proverbs and their relevance to the interpretation of the Book of Mormon, other Wisdom literature may be relevant and fruitful for interpreting Nephi's writings.

33. Raymond C. Van Leeuwen, "Liminality and Worldview in Proverbs 1–9," *Semeia* 50 (1990), 111–144; Carole R. Fontaine, "The Sage in Family and Tribe," in *The Sage in Israel and the Ancient Near East*, ed. John G. Gammie and Leo G. Perdue (Winona Lake, IN: Eisenbrauns, 1990), 158–163; Michael V. Fox, "The Social Location of the Book of Proverbs," in *Texts, Temple, and Traditions: A Tribute to Menahem Haran*, eds. Michael V. Fox, et al. (Winona Lake, IN: Eisenbrauns, 1996), 227–239; Richard J. Clifford, "The Community of the Book of Proverbs," in *Constituting the Community: Studies on the Polity of Ancient Israel in Honor of S. Dean McBride, Jr.*, eds. John T. Strong and Steven S. Tuell (Winona Lake, IN: Eisenbrauns, 2005), 281–293; Stuart Weeks, *An Introduction to the Study of Wisdom Literature* (London: T&T Clark, 2010).

34. What protestant Christians call the Old Testament is often called the Hebrew Bible by scholars.

35. The Wisdom tradition word *knowledge* appears in these Proverbs passages: 1:4; 1:7; 1:22; 1:29; 2:5–6; 2:10; 3:20; 5:2; 8:9–10; 8:12; 9:10; 10:14; 11:9; 12:1; 12:23; 13:16; 14:6–7; 14:18; 15:2; 15:7; 15:14; 17:27; 18:15; 19:2; 19:25; 19:27; 20:15; 21:11; 22:12; 22:17; 22:20; 23:12; 24:4–5; 29:7; 30:3.

36. For other examples of how deeply interpretable 1 Nephi 1 can be, see *A Dream, A Rock, and a Pillar of Fire: Reading 1 Nephi 1*, Adam Miller, ed. (Provo, UT: Neal A. Maxwell Institute for Religious Scholarship), 2017; *of Latter-day Saint Faith and Scholarship* (2014) at https://interpreterfoundation. org/another-suggestion-for-reading-1-nephi-1-1-3/; Neal Rappleye "Nephi the Good: A Commentary 1 Nephi 1:1–3," *Interpreter: A Journal of Latter-day Saint Faith and Scholarship* (2014) at https://www.mormoninterpreter.com/ nephi-the-good-a-commentary-on-1-nephi-11–3/.

37. It is not new to read Wisdom themes in the Book of Mormon. Still, there is much more yet to be discovered. Some of the scholars who have previously

mined portions of the Book of Mormon for Wisdom themes include: Hugh Nibley, *The Prophetic Book of Mormon* (Salt Lake City: Deseret Book and FARMS, 1989); Daniel C. Peterson, "Nephi and His Asherah: A Note on 1 Nephi 11:8–23," in *Mormons, Scripture, and the Ancient World: Studies in Honor of John L. Sorenson,* ed. Davis Bitton (Provo, UT: FARMS, 1998), 191–243; Kevin Christensen, "Nephi, Wisdom, and the Deuteronomist Reform," *Insights 23/2* (2003), 2–3; Kevin Christensen, "Jacob's Connections to First Temple Traditions," *Insights* 23/4 (2003), 2–3; Kevin Christensen, "The Temple, the Monarchy, and Wisdom: Lehi's World and the Scholarship of Margaret Barker," in *Glimpses of Lehi's Jerusalem,* eds. John W. Welch, David Rolph Seely, and Jo Ann H. Seely (Provo, UT: FARMS, 2004), 449–522; Alyson Skabelund Von Feldt, "Does God Have a Wife?" *FARMS Review* 19/1 (Provo, UT: Maxwell Institute, 2007), 81–118; Alyson Skabelund Von Feldt, "'His Secret Is with the Righteous': Instructional Wisdom in the Book of Mormon," Occasional Papers: Number 5 (Provo, UT: Maxwell Institute, 2007). The particular piece by Skabelund Von Feldt may currently be the most focused and thorough investigation of the Book of Mormon through the lens of Wisdom.

38. See Michael P. Streck and Nathan Wasserman, "Mankind's Bitter Fate: The Wisdom Dialog Bm 79111+," *Journal of Cuneiform Studies,* 66 (2014), 39–47, especially p. 40; Michael P. Streck, "Schilf" [= "Reed"] in *Reallexikon der Assyriologie und Vorderasiatischen Archäologie,* Bd. 12/3–4 (2009), 182–89, especially p. 188.

39. I put *fear* in parentheses to remind readers that these terms are interchangeable in the Wisdom tradition. Proverbs states, "The fear of the Lord is the beginning of knowledge" (Proverbs 1:7).

40. Noel B. Reynolds, "Nephi's Outline," in *Book of Mormon Authorship: New Light on Ancient Origins,* ed. Noel B. Reynolds (Provo, UT: Religious Studies Center, Brigham Young University, 1982), 53–74.

41. Unfortunately, Lemuel was one of the great fools of the Book of Mormon because he chose to hearken to the words of another fool, Laman, rather than the words of the wise, Nephi or Lehi. "It is better to hear the rebuke of the wise, than for a man to hear the song of fools" (Ecclesiastes 7:5). "And it came to pass that Laman was angry with me, and also with my father; and also was Lemuel, for he hearkened unto the words of Laman. Wherefore Laman and Lemuel did speak many hard words unto us, their younger brothers, and they did smite us even with a rod" (1 Nephi 3:28). In condemning Laman and Lemuel as fools who spoke "many hard words," we remember that the Wisdom tradition teaches that "a fool's voice *is known* by multitude of words" (Ecclesiastes 5:3).

42. For a biblical story of paronomasia involving the name *Nabal*, see the story of David, Abigail, and Nabal in 1 Samuel 25.

43. See for example Alan Goff, "Scratching the Surface of Book of Mormon Narratives," *FARMS Review of Books* 12/2 (2000), especially pp. 18–19.

44. For another literary interpretation of Laban's death, see Steven L. Olsen, "The Death of Laban: A Literary Interpretation," *The FARMS Review* 21/1 (2009), 179–195.

45. 1 Nephi 4:13–17 provides a justification for killing Laban that may evoke themes from the Wisdom tradition (remember that Nephi is the wise man and Laban is the fool). See for example Proverbs 1:24–32; 2:12–15, 22; 3:33–35; 4:19; 5:22–23; 6:12–15; 8:36; 11:3, 8, 19, 21, 28, 31; 12:6–7, 21; 13:9; 14:11; 15:10–11; 16:6; 19:9; 21:25, 28; 24:17–18; 28:10, 18.

46. Though what follows is a very limited list, Wisdom themes seem to prevail throughout the Book of Mormon. A cursory review of the Book of Mormon seems to connect in these ways. Theme 1, listening to and recording the words of his wise father—some potential passages to explore include Jacob 1; Enos 1; Jarom 1; Omni 1; Mosiah 6; Helaman 5; Alma 36–42; Mormon 1, Moroni 7. Theme 2, valuing learning and education—Enos 1; Mosiah 1; Mosiah 2; Mormon 1. Theme 3, embracing hard work—Jacob 1; Enos 1; Jarom 1; Alma 43; Moroni 9. Theme 4, seeking understanding from the Lord despite suffering and trials—Jacob 3, Enos 1; Record of Zeniff (Mosiah 9–22); Alma 14; Moroni 9. Theme 5, demonstrating the difference between the wise man and the fool—Jacob 2–3; Mosiah 2–5; Alma 46 and 48. Or, following the pattern we saw with Nephi and Laban, one might also ask, "How does Jacob represent the wise man and Sherem the fool?"; "How does Alma the Younger represent the wise man and Korihor the fool?"; "How does Noah and the priests of Noah represent the fool and Abinadi the wise man?"; "How does Alma the Younger represent the wise man and Nehor the fool?"; "How does Amalickiah, or Ammoron, represent the fool and Captain Moroni the wise man?" Another theme in Wisdom literature is the advice for the wise man to avoid alluring women. How does Corianton represent the foolish son and his father represent the wise father? These and many other Wisdom themes and questions should prove fruitful for Book of Mormon scholarship.

47. This chapter was originally published as "Becoming a Man of God Like Nephi" with my co-author Ryan Brower on DeseretNews.com at https://www.deseretnews.com/article/865638713/Nephi-becomes-a-man.html. It is republished with permission.

48. This chapter was originally published "Evidences for the Book of Mormon: In Cover of Darkness and the Turning of the New Year" on DeseretNews.com at https://www.deseretnews.com/article/865618775/Evidences-for-the-Book-

of-Mormon-In-cover-of-darkness-and-the-turning-of-the-New-Year.html. It is republished with permission.

49. This chapter was originally published as "What We Know About One of the Most Prominent Mothers Mentioned in the Book of Mormon" with my co-author Camille Fronk Olson on LDSLiving.com at http://www.ldsliving.com/What-We-Know-About-One-of-the-Most-Prominent-Mothers-Mentioned-in-the-Book-of-Mormon/s/85361. It is republished with permission.

50. This chapter was originally published as "Finding the First Use of the Name Christ in the Book of Mormon" on DeseretNews.com at https://www.deseretnews.com/article/865647065/Finding-the-first-use-of-the-name-Christ-in-the-Book-of-Mormon.html?pg=all. It is republished with permission.

51. This chapter was originally published as "1 Nephi 12-14. Nephi's Grand Vision" at InterpreterFoundation.org at https://interpreterfoundation.org/res-1-nephi-12-14-nephis-grand-vision/. It is republished with permission.

52. For more connections between Apocalyptic literature and Book of Mormon texts see Mark Thomas, "Lehi's Dream: An American Apocalypse," paper presented at the Fourth Annual Symposium of The Association for Mormon Letters, BYU, Provo, Utah, October 13, 1979, available at http://mldb.byu.edu/thomas.htm.

53. In the original Greek the word *history* refers to a thorough inquiry and examination for the purpose of learning.

54. These four themes are adapted from the suggestions of Rulon Eames, "First Book of Nephi" *Encyclopedia of Mormonism*, ed. Daniel Ludlow (New York: Macmillan Publishing Company, 1992), 146.

55. The term *Gentile* in its original Hebrew context means "nations," hence "foreigner, stranger, other." It does not necessarily mean "non-Jew." Nephi uses this meaning of the term to refer to Christopher Columbus as a foreigner, a non-Nephite, and a non-Lamanite.

56. This chapter was originally published as "2 Nephi 1: Resurrecting Deep Sleepers" at InterpreterFoundation.org at https://interpreterfoundation.org/res-2-nephi-1-resurrecting-deep-sleepers/. It is republished with permission.

57. See Genesis 1; John 1:1–5; Moses 2-3; Abraham 4–5 (notice in Moses 3:21 and Abraham 5:14 that Adam was in a "deep sleep" before Eve was presented to him). The theme of a god speaking and creation responding is also seen in ancient Egyptian literature. The Memphite creation account records that all things were brought into being by the word of the god Ptah. The word *Ptah* means "to open," as in opening the mouth to speak. And, for fun, the word *EgyPT* derives from the name of this ancient, famous EgyPTian god, Ptah (I put in caps the portion of the word *EgyPT* that derives from the name *Ptah*)

*The Ancient Near East Volume 1: An Anthology of Texts and Pictures*, James B. Pritchard ed. (Princeton: Princeton University Press), 1958, 1–2.

58. *The Brown-Driver-Briggs Hebrew and English Lexicon*, (Oxford: Oxford University Press), 1952, 922.

59. *The Brown-Driver-Briggs Hebrew and English Lexicon*, 922.

60. *The Brown-Driver-Briggs Hebrew and English Lexicon*, 734–735. It must be recognized that *ur* is a different Hebrew root word for light that is found in the phrase *urim and thummim* (which means something like "light and truth").

61. *The Brown-Driver-Briggs Hebrew and English Lexicon*, 922. Arabic, a sister language to Hebrew, also has a word like *radam* that is pronounced *radama*; it means "to stop up (door, gap, etc.) whence perhaps *be deaf* (stopped up to sounds, etc)."

62. This chapter was originally published as "'O How Great the Goodness of Our God': 2 Nephi 6-10" on InterpreterFoundation.org at https://interpreterfoundation.org/res-o-how-great-the-goodness-of-our-god-2-nephi-6-10/. It is republished with permission.

63. This chapter was originally published as "Reflections on Symbolism in the Atonement" on DeseretNews.com at https://www.deseretnews.com/article/865668511/Reflections-on-symbolism-in-the-Atonement.html?pg=all. It is republished with permission.

64. This chapter was originally published as "One Simple Tool to Help You Get So Much More Out of Isaiah" on LDSLiving.com at http://www.ldsliving.com/The-Silence-of-Isaiah-in-the-Book-of-Mormon/s/84704. It is republished with permission.

65. For an excellent resource on parallelism identified throughout the Book of Mormon, see Donald W. Parry, *Poetic Parallelisms in the Book of Mormon* (Provo, Utah: Neal A. Maxwell Institute for Religious Scholarship), 2007.

66. This chapter was originally published as "Jacob 1–4: Seek the Kingdom of God" on InterpreterFoundation.org at https://interpreterfoundation.org/res-jacob-1-4-seek-the-kingdom-of-god/. It is republished with permission.

67. This chapter was originally published as "'Wrestling' for Answers: 5 People from Scriptures Who Asked Difficult Question" on LDSLiving.com at http://www.ldsliving.com/-Wrestling-for-Answers-5-People-from-the-Scriptures-Who-Asked-Difficult-Questions/s/85300. It is republished with permission.

68. This chapter was originally published as "Mosiah 4-6: Children of Christ" on InterpreterFoundation.org at https://interpreterfoundation.org/res-mosiah-4-6-children-of-christ/. It is republished with permission.

69. Stephen Ricks, "Kingship, Coronation, and Covenant in Mosiah 1-6" in *King Benjamin's Speech: "That Ye May Learn Wisdom"* ed. John W. Welch and Stephen D. Ricks (FARMS: Provo, 1998), 255–256.

70. This chapter was originally published as "Mosiah 12–16: Martyr in Disguise" on InterpreterFoundation.org at https://interpreterfoundation.org/res-mosiah-12-16-martyr-in-disguise/. It is republished with permission.

71. Taylor Halverson, "Martyrdom of Isaiah" *Encyclopedia of Ancient History*, 2013.

72. Walter Bauer, *A Greek-English Lexicon of the New Testament and Other Early Christian Literature*, 2nd ed., trans. William F. Arndt and F. Wilbur Gingrich (Chicago: University of Chicago Press, 1979), 494.

73. This is likely a sign of the ancient literary feature of word play, also known as paronomasia or midrashic punning.

74. *The Brown-Driver-Briggs Hebrew and English Lexicon*, 626. The root of *nadi* is *nud*. Because we do not have the original Hebrew text (or Reformed Egyptian text for that matter), it is impossible to determine the exact root word. Other root words as *nadad* (to wander, to flee, to retreat) or *nadah* (to put away, exclude) are other possible options in the name *Abinadi* and fit the context of the story as well. The evidence suggests that the Book of Mormon is engaged in paronomasia (punning and word play), an ancient literary feature that demonstrated authorial artistic sophistication and beauty.

75. Compare this story to that of Brigham Young's succession to the presidency of the Church after the death of the Prophet Joseph Smith. Benjamin Ashby recorded, "I was in the congregation when the question of succession to the leadership of the Church was before the people and I solemnly assert and testify that the last time I saw the features, the gestures, and heard the sound of the voice of Joseph Smith was when the form, voice and countenance of Brigham Young was transfigured before the congregation so that he appeared like Joseph Smith in every particular. Thus the Lord showed his people that the mantle of Joseph had been bestowed upon Brigham." This quote and additional information of interest is found in *The Autobiography of Parley P Pratt, Revised and Enhanced Edition*, ed. Scot Facer Proctor and Maurine Jensen Proctor (Salt Lake City: Deseret Book, 2000), 419, footnote 12.

76. *The Brown-Driver-Briggs Hebrew and English Lexicon*, 68. The Hebrew word underlying the English text is *ba'afer* from the root word *'afer*. This same word can also be translated as "bandage" (see for example the New Revised Standard Version translation of 1 Kings 20:38).

77. *The HarperCollins Study Bible: New Revised Standard Version*, ed. Wayne E. Meeks (New York: HarperCollins Publishers, 1993), 554, footnote 20:38.

78. This chapter was originally published as "How Suffering Is Good for Us and How it Can Make Us Happy" on LDSLiving.com at http://www.ldsliving.com/Why-Suffering-is-Good-for-Us-and-How-it-Can-Make-Us-Happy/s/87187. It is republished with permission.

79. This chapter was originally published as "Evidences for the Book of Mormon: Why the Missionary Zeal of Abish" on DeseretNews.com at https://www.deseretnews.com/article/865630202/Evidences-for-the-Book-of-Mormon-Why-the-missionary-zeal-of-Abish.html?pg=all. It is republished with permission.

80. *Lectures on Faith* (Salt Lake City, UT: Deseret Book, 1985), 38.

81. This idea was shared with me by Dr. Matt Bowen.

82. This chapter was originally published at "The Greek Meaning of Conversion that Will Deepen Your Understanding of What It Means to Come Unto Christ" on LDSLiving.com at http://www.ldsliving.com/The-Greek-Meaning-of-Conversion-That-Will-Deepen-Your-Understanding-of-What-It-Means-to-Come-Unto-Christ/s/87188. It is republished with permission.

83. This chapter was originally published as "Why God Calls His People 'Strangers' (+What it Has to Do with Covenants) on LDSLiving.com at http://www.ldsliving.com/Why-God-Calls-His-People-Strangers-What-It-Has-to-Do-with-Covenants/s/84551. It is republished with permission.

84. This chapter was originally published as "Evidences for the Book of Mormon: In Cover of Darkness and the Turning of the New Year" on DeseretNews.com at http://www.deseretnews.com/article/865618775/Evidences-for-the-Book-of-Mormon-In-cover-of-darkness-and-the-turning-of-the-New-Year.html. It is republished with permission.

85. This chapter was originally published as "What Does God Really Mean When He Says 'Be of Good Cheer'?" on LDSLiving.com at http://www.ldsliving.com/What-Does-God-Mean-When-He-Says-Be-of-Good-Cheer/s/84926. It is republished with permission.

86. This chapter was originally published as "3 Nephi 7: A Reflection on Human Unrighteousness" on InterpreterFoundation.org at https://interpreterfoundation.org/res-3-nephi-7-a-reflection-upon-human-unrighteousness/. It is republished with permission.

87. This chapter was originally published as "3 Nephi 17-19: Christ's Visit to the Americas" on InterpreterFoundation.org at https://interpreterfoundation.org/res-3-nephi-17-19-christs-visit-to-the-americas/. It is republished with permission.

88. This chapter was originally published as "What Does it Mean that Mormon Was Quick to Observe?" on LDSLiving.com at http://www.ldsliving.com/What-Does-It-Mean-that-Mormon-Was-Quick-to-Observe/s/85069. It is republished with permission.

89. This chapter was originally published as "Mormon 1–9: I Write that Ye Might Believe in the Gospel of Jesus Christ" on InterpreterFoundation.org https://interpreterfoundation.org/res-mormon-1-9-i-write-that-ye-might-believe-the-gospel-of-jesus-christ/. It is republished with permission.

90. See also 1 Nephi 8:28; 11:7; Mosiah 4:11; Alma 32:35; 36:26.

91. See also 1 Nephi 4:3; Alma 1:2; Helaman 1:15; Ether 1:34; 14:10.

92. This chapter was originally published as "2 Undeniable Truths that Will Bring Us Joy During Bitter Trials" on LDSLiving.com at http://www.ldsliving.com/2-Undeniable-Truths-That-Will-Bring-Us-Joy-During-Bitter-Trials/s/85068. It is republished with permission.

93. Spencer W. Kimball, *Faith Precedes the Miracle* (Salt Lake City, UT: Deseret Book, 1972), 98.

94. This chapter was originally published as "How Biblical Sacrifices Connect to Today's Sacrament" on DeseretNews.com at https://www.deseretnews.com/article/865671522/How-biblical-sacrifices-connect-to-todays-sacrament.html. It is republished with permission.

95. This chapter was originally published as "The Surprising Story of a Book of Mormon in the Harvard Library" on DeseretNews.com at https://www.deseretnews.com/article/865651869/The-surprising-story-of-a-Book-of-Mormon-in-the-Harvard-library.html?pg=all. It is republished with permission.

96. This chapter was originally published as "Forgiveness Is to Abandon All Hope of a Better Past and Why That Builds a Better Future" on LDSLiving.com at http://www.ldsliving.com/Forgiveness-Is-to-Abandon-All-Hope-of-a-Better-Past-and-Why-That-Builds-a-Better-Future/s/85314. It is republished with permission.

97. Brent Strong, Mark Davis, and Taylor Halverson, *History of Creativity in the Arts, Science, & Technology, PRE-1500,* 3rd ed. (Dubuque, IA: Kendall Hunt Publishing, 2014); Brent Strong, Mark Davis, and Taylor Halverson, *History of Creativity in the Arts, Science, & Technology, POST-1500,* 3rd ed. (Dubuque, IA: Kendall Hunt Publishing, 2014).

98. President Dieter F. Uchtdorf, "Happiness, Your Heritage," *Ensign*, November 2008.

99. This quote is attributed to Lily Tomlin.

# ABOUT THE AUTHOR

TAYLOR HALVERSON IS A TEACHING and learning consultant at Brigham Young University; a member of the Book of Mormon Central executive committee; a columnist for the *Deseret News*; a founder of the BYU Creativity, Innovation, and Design group; a travel leader to Mesoamerica and the Holy Land; and the chief innovation officer at Vereo Training.

At BYU, Taylor has taught Book of Mormon, Old Testament, history of creativity, innovation boot camp, basic entrepreneurship skills, and an interdisciplinary design course called "Illuminating the Scriptures: Designing Innovative Study Tools."

Taylor received a BA in ancient Near Eastern studies from BYU, an MA in Biblical studies from Yale, an MS in instructional systems technology from Indiana University, a PhD in instructional systems technology from Indiana University, and a PhD in Judaism and Christianity in antiquity from Indiana University.

He has published and presented widely on scripture, technology, teaching, and learning. For more, check out taylorhalverson.com.